ADVANCE PRAISE
POWERFUL QUESTIONS IN THE BIBLE

★ ★ ★

"The relational focus and fulcrum in *Powerful Questions* is patently timely and urgently needed amidst the plethora of challenges the church faces today. This guided and interactive study is an insightful reminder that the Bible is principled, practical, and probing."

**—Rev. Dr. T.D. Stubblefield, founder & CEO,
T. D. Stubblefield Ministries, LLC; pastor emeritus,
First Baptist Church of Chesterfield**

"*Powerful Questions* are not necessarily those whose answers by research and study we come to know… but those that cause us to look within…to examine heart and soul and mind to find…those that prick and prod us and won't let go…until we not only come to know the answer but in doing so to better know ourselves."

**—Dr. Kathy Hood Culmer, D.Min., author,
professional storyteller, and Christian educator**

"It is with great pleasure that I recommend this insightful and practical guide for spiritual growth. Royce Sutton brings a group of studies that will enlighten and then lead the person to a deeper knowledge of who God is and what a practicing follower looks like. He provides you with enough exegete to inform but more applicational inquiry to force you to go deeper in your thinking of what God will have us to do. You will find yourself wanting more and more with each study lesson. Royce has provided an enlightening gem of insight. You will come away seeking a more substantive relationship with God and humankind."

**—Rev. Adrian Brooks, senior pastor,
McClures Memorial Baptist Church; CEO, Memorial CDC**

AN 11-LESSON STUDENT WORKBOOK &
COMPREHENSIVE FACILITATOR'S GUIDE

Powerful Questions in the Bible

A STUDY OF GOD'S VOICE SPEAKING TO HIS PEOPLE

ROYCE SUTTON

Uriel Press
a division of UMI

Published in the United States by Uriel Press
P.O. Box 436987
Chicago, IL 60643
urielpress.com

ISBN 978-0-9601047-9-6 (paperback)
ISBN 978-0-9993326-9-6 (eBook)

Cover design by Laura Duffy
Book design by Amit Dey

Printed in the United States of America

CONTENTS

★ ★ ★

Appendix

PREFACE

★ ★ ★

This ***Powerful Questions*** study was inspired by a dear friend who preached a sermon about the times when life's questions may not have ready answers. He spoke of those times when we may wrestle with our spiritual purpose or when we may feel the gloom of defeat. In these times of uncertainty, he urged that, conversely, before making a poor life choice or before giving up all together, we should consider that God may, in fact, be asking us ***Powerful Questions:*** Do you love Me? Do you trust Me? Do you confidently know that I have secured the victory before the battle is waged?

At that very moment, my spirit was so taken by this timely, God-inspired message that I hurriedly scratched on a spare piece of paper no less than 15 key, ***Powerful Questions*** from scripture. I was convinced that God was purposefully bringing these questions to my awareness, so that I could hear His voice in these questions being posed at a critical time. These questions, from the New and Old Testaments, reflect God's committed love and are pragmatic openings for His people to make critical choices to reciprocate our love for Him. When God beckoned, "Adam, where art thou?" (Genesis 3:9 KJV), that was, and is, a ***Powerful Question***. Or even still, when Jesus asked His disciples, "But who do you say I am," the question evokes a profound consideration and response based on one's personal encounter with Christ.

Each ***Powerful Question*** in this study was carefully selected to kindle a mutual exchange of deeper study and a personal inventory of spiritual growth that advances the Christian perspective on many of today's important topics, such as righteous living in compromised times, self-control, principled decision-making, and faith-centered leadership preparation.

Know, too, that there are other reflective ***Powerful Questions*** that may require no immediate reply. In those instances, true to Jesus' teaching style, the question itself is the answer. "Where are your accusers? Didn't even one of them condemn you?" Jesus asked the woman who faced a "righteous, religious" stone-thirsty mob for her alleged sin (John 8:10 NLT).

Receive this study, ***Powerful Questions in the Bible,*** and be blessed as I have been. Use it, too, to be a blessing. Use it to be a powerful witness for the Kingdom in your study or as a part of your participation in a facilitated study group. I pray that as you seek guidance from the Holy Spirit to help you answer your own personal ***Powerful Questions,*** you will be led to answers that will prosper you in all your ways and in all good works.

INTRODUCTION

★ ★ ★

We can learn so much from a well-placed, probing, intentional question. A high-quality question provides the receiver an opportunity for clarification and to receive additional information. It, too, may mark the beginning of a personal quest toward wisdom and personal growth, and even still, a question may cause us to reconsider the path of a decision or the future of a relationship. The Bible asks more than 1,700 questions. Some are so powerful that their answers have reshaped the course of history, while others have transformed the lives of spiritual giants, such as the Apostle Paul, the Prophet Jeremiah, the faithful servant Martha, and a condemned man who hung on the cross with Jesus during the final hours of his life.

In *Powerful Questions in the Bible: A Study of God's Voice Speaking to His People,* together we will spend two units and eleven lessons examining select biblical questions that were powerful at the seminal moment they were asked and that remain just as powerful now. The *Powerful Questions* study allows us to consider why the questions were posed, what responses were provided and how those questions may speak to our own personal journeys toward revelation and maturity in God's Word. To seek answers for ourselves in the *Powerful Questions* is our aim. Ponder each question in your study time, allowing the Holy Spirit to give insight and perspective. He will speak to your needs as you experience His Word. Then, use what you have experienced to prepare for your study group gathering. Assuredly, your group gathering will be a powerful time of shared learning, encouragement, and growth.

Powerful Questions is both a personal and a collective study that will bring new insight each time you experience it. Though the study has a common overall theme, each lesson stands on its own for individual and group study. *Powerful Questions* is purposefully styled to challenge us to become stronger spiritually in these uncertain times—times when our own powerful questions may not have ready answers. Trust that God sees you and hears you and that He has an answer for you in all seasons and in all trials. Trust that He stands ready to aid you through weighted burdens, strained relationships, personal doubts, and even as you endure life's storms.

Make each lesson your very own as powerful answers emerge from the ***Powerful Questions*** to create a new powerful step in your spiritual journey, your relationship with the Lord, and your renewed walk in His Word.

Disclosure: Scripture references within ***Powerful Questions*** incorporate multiple sourced Bible translations, as well as the author's interpretive perspective. No two people read or feel Scripture identically, but drawing from diverse biblical translations can provide greater linguistic clarity, deepen and broaden the reader's interpretive lens, and germinate the quest for personal scriptural discovery.

Powerful Questions
Lesson Goals

1. To ***Inspire*** a personal, deeper study of God's Word that kindles a quest for additional insight and personal growth compelled by ***Powerful Questions***.

2. To ***Encourage*** personal reflection and life application from an Old and New Testament ***Powerful Questions*** study.

3. To ***Enlighten*** the content and context surrounding impactful biblical ***Powerful Questions*** with an aim to ***Elevate*** contemporary Godly living with a guided, inductive Bible study.

How to Effectively Use the *Powerful Questions* Study Lessons

1. Select a study time when you are most alert and free of distractions.

2. Begin each lesson study time with a prayer for **u**nderstanding, insight and application.

3. Read through each lesson and then look up the Scripture references provided and read the surrounding verses for background and context.

4. Use reference materials such as concordances, other Bible translations, Bible dictionaries, and related resources and study tools.

5. Know the aim for each lesson as you complete the study materials and reference the aim during your study discoveries.

6. Complete the "Examining the Text" questions and read the accompanying Scriptures for each question, to aide you in broadening your biblical perspective and insight.

7. Identify and circle or highlight the "Examining the Text" questions that speak powerfully to something you have personally experienced or are experiencing now in your walk with God and your other relationships.

8. Facilitators have been given *guided* answers for each "Examining the Text" question.

9. Take notes of your personal insights as you read supporting Scriptures and keep all notes organized in one notebook or electronic ***Powerful Questions*** file.

10. Consider and plan how you will use the "Lesson Application" as your Word in action for adjusting your personal thoughts and deeds so that you become an example of the living Word.

11. Though not required, shared discussion about the material adds great value to the learning experience. Prepare your answers to each lesson's questions, considering that you can potentially bless others with your insight. Remember in group settings to share the mic, though.

12. Complete the final class, "Student Experience Inventory," so that each experience is improved based on your feedback.

Powerful Questions in the Bible

A Study of God's Voice Speaking to His People

UNIT I

MY BROTHER'S KEEPER?

Genesis 4:9

Lesson Aim

To know that we are to bring our offerings for the Lord with joy and with proper measure. To know that jealousy and anger produce sin. To know that God can still speak to us in the middle of unconfessed sin and separation.

Lesson Background

The brothers Cain, a gardener, and Abel, a shepherd, were raised outside of the Garden of Eden by their parents, Adam and Eve. Because of sin, the first earthly family lost the luxury of having their resources abundantly given to them without requiring any effort on their part. However, when their respective possessions increased, they were expected to give an offering that demonstrated respect, gratitude, and thanks for what God had provided. Noteworthy in this story is that God continued to dialogue with His human creation after the original sin and after new sin took root in Cain's heart. This new sin resulted in more sin, tragic sin. How true it is that what takes root in our hearts bears itself in our attitudes, our actions, our words, and our priorities.

Read: Genesis 4:1-13

Powerful Question: Cain asks God, "…Am I my brother's keeper?" (Genesis 4:9 ESV) (God asked Cain what he had done because his brother Abel's blood was crying out to God)

Answer: None given.

Examining the Text

1. What act of worship were Cain and Abel expected to perform? Was there a difference in how the two men carried out their requirement? (vv. 3-5)

—————————————————————————————

—————————————————————————————

—————————————————————————————

—————————————————————————————

2. What can we understand about God's instruction and tone by how He responded to Cain's offering? (vv. 6-7)

—————————————————————————————

—————————————————————————————

—————————————————————————————

—————————————————————————————

3. What was Cain's response when God told him his offering was inadequate? (v.5; 1 Samuel 16:7; Luke 22:31)

—————————————————————————————

—————————————————————————————

—————————————————————————————

—————————————————————————————

4. Was it Cain's perception that God had rejected him, his offering, or both?

> *For the Lord disciplines the one he loves.*
>
> Hebrews 12:6 (ESV)

_____

_____

_____

_____

_____

_____

5. What can we learn from Abel and the sacrifice he chose to give God? (v.4; Luke 6:38)

_____

_____

_____

_____

_____

_____

6. In this lesson, we see that God confronted Cain in his sin. What should be our Godly response if confronted about our sin? (Psalm 139:23-24; 2 Samuel12:13; 1 John 1:8-9; 2 Corinthians 7:9-10)

_____

_____

_____

_____

_____

How many of us want special consideration when our attitude or performance does not meet up to an agreed-upon expectation level?

- *Are we accountable when we fail to meet that standard?*
- *Are we able or willing to accept the consequences that may accompany an attitude or performance failure?*

"Do all things without grumbling or disputing." **Philippians 2:14 (ESV)**

7. How did Cain express his anger toward God, and where did he commit his deed? Is the place where he committed his fatal sin significant? (v. 6-8; 1 John 3:12)

_____

_____

_____

_____

_____

8. How serious, as God confronted Cain, was the blood on the ground? (Leviticus 17:10-14)

_____

_____

_____

_____

_____

9. When God, in verse 9, inquired about what Cain had done, what was Cain's response? What was Cain effectively saying in his response to God?

_____

_____

_____

_____

_____

_____

10. What does it mean to be our brother's or sister's keeper? In what ways can we demonstrate love for others?

_____

_____

_____

_____

_____

_____

11. What more do we learn in verse 13 about Cain's heart?

_____

_____

_____

_____

_____

_____

Things to Remember

- God has a standard of living and giving for His people.

- God wants us to bring our best gifts to him with joy and gladness.

- God provides for us and in return He only asks for a portion to be given back to Him.

- The tenderness of God speaks to us, urging us to do better when we miss the mark.

- We never have to compare ourselves to others as we give and worship.

- God responds.

- A sin-sick life rejects accountability and ownership for deeds of commission and omission.

- We should not ignore God's warning about sin and its plan to take us.

- We can never improve our relationship with God by taking others away from Him.

- Displaced anger has ruined many relationships

- God speaks to us through His Holy Spirit urging us to avoid certain actions and responses.

- Blood is symbolic of life sustained, the liquid spirit of one's life.

Lesson Application

1. **Write the name of one person you have harmed emotionally. Write two things you can do to display love to that person and what you can do to improve your attitude toward him or her.**

   - Pray for your relationships. (e.g., prayers of confession, prayers of accepting God's plan for a relationship, prayers of patience to be willing to love through the difficulty, prayers for God's will to be done, etc.)

2. **Consider whether you are obediently giving back to God what He expects from your time, talent, and treasure. Are you giving with the attitude that demonstrates your joy in giving?**

Supporting Scriptures

- Genesis 9:6 – The penalty for murder is death.
- Leviticus 17:10-14 – The life of a creature is in the blood; the blood gives atonement for the soul.
- 1 Samuel 16:7 – God looks upon the heart.
- Psalm 139:23-24 – Search me, oh God, and know my heart.
- Ephesians 4:32 – Be kind to one another, tender hearted, forgiving one another.
- Mark 7:20-23 – What comes out of a person is what defiles.
- Matthew 15:19 – For out of the heart comes evil thoughts, murders, adulteries…
- Matthew 25:14-30 – The master entrusts his servants with his money while he is away.
- Luke 6:38 – Give and receive back a measure that is pressed down…overflowing.
- Luke 22:31 – …Satan has asked to sift each of you like wheat.
- Luke 10:25-37 – In the parable of the Good Samaritan, Jesus asks who was the most neighborly.
- Hebrews 11:6 – Without faith it is impossible to please God.
- 2 Corinthians 7:9-10 – Godly sorrow brings repentance leading to salvation and leaves no regret.
- 1 John 1:9 – If we confess our sins, He is faithful and just to forgive us of our sin and to cleanse us from all unrighteousness.
- 1 John 3:12 – Cain slew his brother, because his own works were evil, and his brother's works were righteous.
- 1 John 3:15 – Everyone who hates his brother is a murderer, without eternal life abiding in them.

Facts

Cain – First-born child of Adam and Eve, a farmer, poor offerings, angry because God didn't like his offering, advised by God with words of how to do well and what to avoid, slew his brother, was cursed from the ground to be a fugitive and wanderer, given a mark so that others would fear killing him, lived east of the Garden in Nod, had a son (Enoch)

Abel - Second born child, shepherd, brought God a good offering

Next Lesson
"Limit on Forgiveness?"
Matthew 18:21

LIMIT ON FORGIVENESS?

Matthew 18:21

- Are there people in your life with whom you have reached the end of what you can bear?
- Have you dealt with someone who has intentionally attempted to cause you physical, financial, or emotional harm?

Lesson Aim

To know that God's standard for love and forgiveness is rooted in love. To know that Christ's forgiveness model far exceeds the human standards. To appreciate that unlimited forgiveness is a necessary blessing of compassion and unearned redemption for everyone.

Chapter Background

In the previous chapter, Matthew 17, Jesus speaks to His disciples as they seek to know who is the greatest in Heaven. Jesus responds to them about caring for and not misleading innocent children. Then He uses a parable about pursuing one lost sheep while leaving the larger flock. Further, He shares how to first deal with an offending person one-on-one. These are lessons about navigating priority relationships toward the goals of restoration, reconciliation, and unity among believers. His desires were to teach and invoke His presence in all matters, great and small. Next, Jesus shifts their attention to the issue of forgiveness. Peter seeks to know how much extended forgiveness is sufficient when one is offended. Jesus teaches, true to form, with a parable first and then He shares a lesson that destroys any anticipated limits on forgiveness.

Lesson Verses: Matthew 18:15-22

Powerful Question: Matthew 18:21 (ESV)
Then came Peter to him and said, "Lord, how often will my brother sin against me, and I forgive him? As many as seven times?"

Powerful Answer: Matthew 18:22 (ESV)
Jesus said to him, "I do not say to you seven times, but seventy-seven times."

"To err is human, to forgive is divine." Alexander Pope

Forgiveness
Deliberate decision to release feelings of anger, resentment, or vengeance toward someone who has hurt you.

Unforgiveness
Mix of bitterness, hostility, anger, revenge, and fear. A retained grudge that causes the feeling of hurt to reappear. Our peace, trust, comfort, and happiness are compromised.

Jewish Law on Forgiveness - *teshuvah*

- An atoning that includes the offender's cessation of the harmful acts, regret over the action, confession, and repentance.

- The one who hurts another must sincerely apologize three times. If the victim does not accept the offender's apology, then the offender is forgiven and the victim shares blame for the hurt.

- **Rosh Hosanna and Yom Kippur** - Ten days of awe or atonement, to make amends and seek forgiveness from others and God; prayers and fasting to demonstrate sincerity while seeking reconciliation; make amends for shortcomings.

Examining the Text

1. If we look closely at Peter's question in verse 21, what was he asking Jesus?

_____

_____

_____

_____

_____

_____

2. In Peter's question, what was likely his greatest concern? Was it the seriousness of an act committed against him, the number of times an act had been committed, the way he should respond to an offending party, or something else? Further, what should we be most concerned about when we are wronged by another person? (vv. 21 and 15)

_____

_____

_____

_____

_____

_____

3. Was Peter's thinking counter to Christ's teachings and, if so, how? (v. 22; 6:14-15; 5:7)

_____

_____

_____

_____

_____

_____

God of compassion and mercy, slow to get angry and filled with unfailing love and faithfulness .

Psalm 86:15 (NLT)

4. What assurance or guarantees come with forgiving someone? Share your thoughts or concerns about extending forgiveness.

5. When Jesus gave an equation to determine how many times to extend forgiveness (see KJV v. 22), should Peter or we take this number literally?

6. What essential elements are included in forgiveness? (See Genesis 50:17-21)

7. How does forgiveness affect our prayer life? (Mark 11:25; Matthew 5:23-24)

8. What will result from the forgiveness we extend? (Matthew 6:14; Luke 6:37-38; Genesis 50:20-21)

9. On what basis do I have the option to write someone off with no possibility of forgiveness? (Romans 12:1-3; Mark 8:34-35)

10. What can we learn and apply from verses 15-17 that will help us extend forgiveness?

_____

_____

_____

_____

_____

_____

11. Again, why must I forgive?

_____

_____

_____

_____

_____

_____

Things to Remember

- Christians don't have a limit on forgiveness.

- Forgiveness is a process that may require others to intervene.

- Forgiveness is never about the offending party, it's always about me.

- We must forgive with as much grace the one thousandth time as when we forgave the first time. This is only possible with the Spirit of Christ Who lives within us and being mindful that God has forgiven us repeatedly.

- When we consider the degree that we ourselves have been forgiven, how can we not forgive?

- Love is at the heart of forgiveness.

- Restoration is the aim of forgiveness.

- A disrupted relationship among believers impacts more than the two parties.

Lesson Application

1. **Do you have people in your life with whom you have reached the end of what you can bear? List them and how they have hurt you.**

2. **What, then, are your Godly next steps?**

Supporting Scriptures

- Genesis 50:15-21 – First biblical use of the word forgiveness as Joseph's family seeks it for selling him into slavery.

- Leviticus 16:20-22 – Origin of forgiveness: scapegoat. The Hebrew word is *azazel*. The goat carrying collective sins is pushed off a cliff as an absolute removal.

- Leviticus 19:18 – You shall not take vengeance or bear a grudge; love your neighbor as yourself.

- Matthew 5:23-24 – Before offering a gift at the altar, you must go make peace with someone you've offended.

- Matthew 5:40-48 – Go the extra mile even when the person may not "deserve" it.

- Matthew 5:43-48 – "…but I say to you, love your enemies and pray for those who persecute you."

- Matthew 6:12 – Forgive us the wrongs we have done, as we forgive the wrongs that others have done to us.

- Matthew 6:14-15 – If we refuse to forgive others, we will not be forgiven.

- Mark 11:25 – Forgiveness is required before prayer.

- Luke 6:27-36 – Do good to others not expecting anything in return and be merciful as your Father is merciful.

- Luke 17:3-4 – Forgive after repentance, even if the person sins against you seven times a day.

- Luke 23:34 – "Father, forgive them, for they know not what they do."

- Acts 2:38 – Repent and be baptized so that your sins can be forgiven.

- Acts 3:18-20 – Repent so that God will forgive your sins.

- Hebrews 9:15 – Jesus' death enabled redemption.
- 1 John 1:9 – But if we confess our sins to God, He will keep His promise and do what is right; He will forgive your sins and purify you from all your wrongdoing.
- I John 3:18 – Love each other by your actions and not mere words.
- Ephesians 4:31-32 – Get rid of all bitterness and hateful feelings and forgive others just as Christ forgave you.
- Colossians 3:12-13 – The people of God are to make room for others' faults and forgive anyone who has offended us; the Lord forgave.
- James 5:16 – Confess our sins to each other; prayer is powerful.
- 1 Peter 4:8 – And above all things have fervent love for one another.

Jesus Adds More About Forgiveness (Matthew 18:23-35)

In the parable of the unmerciful servant, Jesus insists we must be in the full-time forgiveness business. In a later parable, Jesus supports His answer with v. 33-35. "Shouldn't you have mercy on your fellow servant, just as I have mercy on you? In anger, his master handed him over to the jailers to be tortured, until he should pay back all he owed. That's what my heavenly Father will do to you if you refuse to forgive your brothers and sisters from your heart."

Types of Forgiveness[1]

A. *Exoneration* – The slate is wiped clean, completely. Full restoration happens when one is taken back to a position of innocence. Forgive and forget. The offense could have come from an accidental incident. Or, the offender was a child or someone who was unable to grasp the extent of their actions. The offender is truly sorry for their known and admitted action, are apologetic, and have the full intent of not repeating the offense.

---

1. Roes, Debbie. "On Forgiveness: The Three Types and When They Apply," ar3cle based on a lecture by Steve Marmer at Prager University, published on April 26, 2018, My Wardrobe, Myself blog, hQps://mywardrobemyself.com/2018/04/26/three-types-of-forgiveness/.

B. *Forbearance* – The offending party makes a partial apology or believes that you are partially to blame for the offense. Occurs in an important relationship and maintaining it is more important than the offense. Grudges and revenge are not considerations. May warrant keeping a watchful, cautious eye on the person to ensure a pattern does not develop.

C. *Release* – This is the lowest degree of forgiveness for those who have never acknowledged or apologized for their wrong or when the apology was insincere. The offender makes no attempt to repair, reconcile, or reimburse from the incident. The relationship no longer needs to continue. In turn, the victim must let go of all the hurtful feelings associated with that person and the incident and instead commit to whatever care is needed to free the mind and heart from the offender, the incident(s), and the associated trauma.

Next Lesson
"What About Leading Your Own?"
1 Timothy 3:5

"WHAT ABOUT LEADING YOUR OWN?"

1 Timothy 3:5

★ ★ ★

Lesson Aim:

To know that church leaders meet standards prior to assuming a leadership role, and that those same standards remain after assuming that role. To know that one's reputation is a result of deeds and words that reveal one's character and readiness for leadership within the body of believers. To know that leadership standards are not only for those desiring leadership, but they also apply to all believers.

Lesson Background

Paul wrote this first letter to Timothy, other young church leaders, and believers everywhere at about A.D. 64. It was written so that the early church would be foundationally solid and orderly regarding conduct, lifestyle, and leadership. In particular, our study passage targets bishops, pastors, church leaders, and elders of the local church. Also, further in chapter 3, Paul outlines the standards for those who desire the office of deacon. The spiritual character of a church's leadership is so very important toward building a healthy fellowship of believers. Careful, considered selection of church leaders is paramount to creating a foundation for our churches to mature and thrive. As well, according to A.W. Tozer, the pursuit of holiness extends from "the pool, pulpit, pew, and porch."

Read: 1 Timothy 3:1-7

Powerful Question: "…how can he take care of God's church?" (1 Timothy 3:5 NLT)

Examining the Text

1. Those desiring to be church leaders should know that church work is good work, but there are requirements. The first requirement is outlined in verse 2. What is it and what does it mean? (Titus 1:7-8; Acts 20:28; 1 Timothy 4:12)

    _____

    _____

    _____

    _____

> *For all have sinned and come short of the glory of God.*
>
> *Romans 3:23 (KJV)*

2. Is the blameless standard too high of a bar for anyone? How can it be reached? (2 Corinthians 13:11; 2 Peter 1:5-8)

    _____

    _____

    _____

3. Verse 2 speaks of leader qualifications that include temperance, sober-mindedness, and good behavior. How do these qualifications impact a church's effort to create one-mindedness?

    _____

    _____

    _____

4. List other leader-qualifying characteristics described in verses 2 and 3, and share how they aid a maturing, Christ-centered church.

_____

_____

_____

_____

_____

_____

5. How are the leader characteristics mentioned in verses 4 and 5 different from those in verses 1-3? Why is this significant?

_____

_____

_____

_____

_____

_____

6. The theme of verse 5 centers on how effective one is at managing their household as a qualifier for leadership. Is this a fair measure? Explain.

_____

_____

_____

_____

_____

7. Is a home led by fear and authority an indication that a person is effectively leading their household based on verses 4 and 5? Is the effective household the one that brings harmony with respected boundaries? Share your perspective on what makes for a Christ-centered household.

8. Do these verses disqualify a person from leadership if any member of their household is living an immoral or rebellious life?

9. Leadership qualifications continue in verses 6 and 7. Share how these requirements are important. (2 Timothy 2:24-26; 2 Corinthians 8:21)

> *I press toward the mark for the prize of the high calling of God in Christ Jesus.*
>
> *Philippians 3:14 (KJV)*

10. If a believer never plans to be a church leader, do the leadership standards still apply? (James 3:13,17)

_____

_____

_____

_____

_____

_____

Things to Remember

- Desiring to be a leader is a good thing and should be encouraged.
- We should consider God's standard as a loving mark for excellence.
- A high standard governing church leaders aids the greater body of believers.
- Leaders are developed and trained for service; so, the church has an obligation to prepare its future leaders and hold its existing leaders accountable.
- Leadership requires humility, love for people and God's church, and consistency.
- Personal habits can disqualify a person from leadership.
- The standards reflect God wanting ministry to be carried by those who are unfettered by life's snares, who are best able to be an example of the Word and do their work with a Godly temperament.

Lesson Application

1. **Pray for our church leaders and provide them essential support so that they will become even better leaders and role models.**

2. **If the Lord has called you to leadership, pray He provides two new ways that you can make your home the place He wants it to be.**

Supporting Scriptures

- 2 Corinthians 8:21 – Be honorable before the Lord. He also wants others to see that we are honorable.

- 2 Corinthians 13:11 – Grow to maturity.

- 1 Timothy 4:12 - Be an example to all believers in living, love, faith, and purity.

- 2 Timothy 2:24-26 – Avoid arguments, be peaceful, be a teacher, and be patient.

- Titus 1:7-8 – Church leaders are not to be arrogant, quick tempered, heavy drinkers, violent, or dishonest with money.

- James 3:13, 17 – Living a life that is wise in God's ways, displays a pattern of good works, and pursues peace, is not only a considerate spirit but is one that demonstrates good works.

- 2 Peter 1:5-8 – To our faith, show moral excellence with knowledge and love for all.

Next Lesson
Matthew 22:36
"What Is Man?"

WHAT IS MAN?

Psalm 8:1-9

Aim

To know that God's acts of creation inherently endow us with great value. To realize that, unlike anything else He created, God considers us special in His sight. To know that we are expected to commit to expressions of appreciation through obedience, giving, and praise.

Lesson Background

Psalm 8 was penned by David as a recognition of God's greatness and His passion for the crowning glory of His created works: humankind. This worship psalm is a recognition of just how close man is to God and how close God is to man. Everything that God created before or after humankind was for humankind's use or care. Humankind's Godly favored status is revealed in the New Testament when humankind, though undeserving, is given God's very best—Jesus Christ.

Read: Psalm 8

Powerful Question: What is man that You are mindful of him, and the son of man that you visit him? (Psalm 8:4 ESV)

Examining the Text

1. In verses 1 and 9, what is the writer attempting to describe when he uses "Lord, our Lord" to open this praise Psalm?

    _____

    _____

    _____

    _____

    _____

    _____

2. What type of name does the Lord have, and how far is His name known? (v.1 and 9; Psalm 113:2; Romans 10:13; Philippians 2:9; Psalm 144:1-2)

    _____

    _____

    _____

    _____

    _____

3. The Lord is described as having a certain kind of name in verses 1 and 9. Why is this type of name so important? (Ecclesiastes 7:1; Proverbs 22:1)

    _____

    _____

    _____

    _____

    _____

4. Why does David seem so awestruck and impressed in verses 3-4? (Genesis 1:26-28; Psalm 145:1-3; Hebrews 2:6-8; Psalm 144:3-4)

_____

_____

_____

_____

_____

5. Where is man's placement in the order of beings created by God? In recognition of His position, what special gift and what assignment has the Lord given to man?

_____

_____

_____

_____

_____

6. What are the three distinct domains for the created things that man is to have rule over? (vv. 6-8)

_____

_____

_____

_____

_____

7. After reviewing verses 6-8, how can we be better stewards over this charge?

_____

_____

_____

_____

_____

_____

8. In what verses do we find references to God having body parts? What are those parts and what are they doing collectively? (KJV)

_____

_____

_____

_____

_____

_____

List of God's Body Parts at Work

1.
_____

2.
_____

3.
_____

Lesson Application

1. **Lift praises to God because He is thinking about you, making you unique and with a purpose. Further, praise Him that He absolutely desires the very best for you.**

2. **Be a voice and participant that cares for the earth and the created resources that God has placed here for humankind to enjoy and maintain.**

Things to Remember

- There is no name above God's name.

- God has a good name that entitles Him to all praise and glory.

- Solely, humankind could choose to reverence Him just for the beauty and perfection of His creation.

- God touched everything He created, and His hands sustain everything that requires power, energy, dormancy, and regeneration.

- God thinks about me, and He visits me, because I am unique and royal in His eyes.

- God gave man gifts, purpose, and works from the very beginning.

Supporting Scriptures

- Genesis 1:26-31 – God makes man in His image, to be like Him and to reign.

- Job 7:17 – What are mere people that You should make so much of us, think of us?

- Proverbs 22:1 – Choose a good reputation over riches gold and silver.

- Eccles. 7:1 – A good reputation is more valuable than costly perfume.

- Psalm 113:2 – Blessed be the name of the Lord, now and forever.

- Psalm 138:8 – The Lord will work out His plan for my life. You made me.

- Psalm 144:1-4 – The Lord is our Rock, Ally, Safe Tower, Shield; He notices us.

- Psalm 145:1-3 – Exalt Him, praise Him! Great is the Lord!

- Romans 10:13 – Call on the name of the Lord and be saved.

- Philippians 2:9 – His name is above every name.

- Romans 10:13 – Everyone who calls on the name of the Lord will be saved.

- Hebrews 2:6-8 – What are mere mortals that You should think about them, care for them?

Next Lesson
John 21:15-17
"Whom Will You Feed?"

WHOM WILL YOU FEED?

John 21:1-19

Aim

To know that Jesus recognized the hour, and He needed His message to be clear. To know that His wounded disciple needed loving encouragement and final instructions. The encouragement demonstrated that mistakes do not have to be a disqualifier to serve. The instructions prioritized the disciple's next ministry phase. And, to know that abounding ministry always begins with and is centered in a love for Christ.

Lesson Background

In John Chapter 20, Jesus makes three post-resurrection appearances. Now, seven of his disciples are on an unsuccessful overnight fishing trip on the Sea of Tiberius (Sea of Galilee) when Jesus, in a fourth sighting, appears on the shoreline. Jesus, early in the morning, calls out to the hungry and frustrated disciples while they are still on their boat. Jesus's kind words are timely and instructional, with guidance for how they will improve their catch. Though they still do not physically recognize Jesus, the disciples follow His instructions; and that choice to follow Him changed their productivity, insight, and ministry focus.

Read: John Chapters 20 and 21

Powerful Question: Speaking directly to Simon Peter with the other disciples present, the Lord asked him three times, "Do you love Me?" (John 21:15-17 NLT)

Examining the Text

1. What happens in verse 6 that showed what can occur when we listen to the correct voice at the right time based on trust and obedience? What can we learn from this?

2. When Jesus appeared to the disciples, was it apparent who He was? (v.7) Among the group, who identified Jesus and what may have helped him recognize that it was the Lord speaking to them? (John 20:2; Luke 5:1-11)

3. In verse 12, what were the disciples fearful of doing, despite having clear knowledge? How can we take the question that they would not ask and use it in our own daily prayer life?

4. After climbing ashore, what were the men specifically conscious of doing with their abundant blessing that Jesus miraculously made happen? (v. 11)

5. Now, Jesus directs His words to only one disciple among the others present. To whom did Jesus direct His words in verses 15-17? Why to him? (Matthew 26:33-35; 16:18-20)

6. How many times did Jesus ask Peter if he loved Him, and earlier during His Passion, how many times did Peter deny knowing Him? (John 13:36-38)

7. Each time Jesus asked Peter about his love, He gave him a specific task to do based on that love. Name each of the tasks and note the differences. (vv. 15-17; Acts 20:27-28)

8. What was Peter's verbal response each time Jesus questioned him in verses 15-17?

Three types of love expressed in vv. 15-17

First time (v. 15) – *Agape* love is volitional, self-sacrificial love. Do you love Jesus more than anyone else? This is referring to the other disciples who were nearby. "If you do, feed My lambs." Our love should cause us to express it, to put feeling into action that meets needs (Hebrews 13:20-21).

Second Time (v. 16) – *Agape* love is volitional, self-sacrificial love. Do you love Jesus with all certainty? It is a love that is not in comparison to or on par with love for others, but is above our love for others. Essentially, be a protector and a caretaker for what Jesus is placing in your ministerial care.

Third Time (v. 17) – *Phileo* love is affection, affinity, or brotherly love. Again, do you love Jesus now that He has asked you to do something of great importance? Your new assignment will require that you give what is needed to sustain life and enable growth.

9. How did Peter feel about being asked the nearly identical question three times in succession in front of the other disciples? Why would Jesus continue to ask Peter the same question?

_____

_____

_____

_____

_____

_____

Things to Remember

- Love for Jesus can take many forms, but it is traceable.
- Some of Jesus's messages were just for His disciples.
- With little time left, Jesus wanted to ensure that His people, from the youngest to the oldest, were cared for.
- Jesus is forgiving.
- The Lord is the Good Shepherd, and He wants us to be good shepherds, too.

Lesson Application

1. **When I think about my love for Jesus, how do I express that love?**
2. **To build upon my love for Jesus, what are ways that I can grow and mature in His love? Lift those up in prayer.**

Supporting Scriptures

- 1 Chronicles 28:9 – Learn to know the God of your ancestors intimately; seek Him.
- 1 Chronicles 29:17 – The Lord examines our hearts.
- 2 Chronicles 6:30 – Forgive Your people, Lord. Give your people what they deserve.

- Jeremiah 17:10 – The Lord searches all hearts; we get our due rewards based on actions.

- Matthew 26:33-35 – Jesus predicts Peter's denial and the other disciples' scattering.

- John 2:24-25 – Jesus didn't trust them because He knew all about them.

- John 10:11 – The Good Shepherd lays down His life for the sheep.

- John 13:36-38 – Jesus predicts Peter's denials.

- Acts 20:27-28 – Be caretakers of yourselves and the flock as shepherds.

- Romans 8:27 – The Father knows all hearts and He wants us believers to act in harmony.

- 1 Thessalonians 2:4 – We are God's approved messengers, to please Him, since He knows our hearts.

- Hebrews 13: 20-21 – The Lord equips those whom He calls to do His will.

- 1 Peter 5: 2-3 – Be shepherds over the flock willingly and not for self-serving purposes.

Next Lesson
James 4:1-2
"The Start of Every Fight"

THE START OF EVERY FIGHT

James 4:1-2

Aim

To know that desires and motives are powerful in any relationship. To know that what is in our heart is manifest in the way we manage ourselves in relationships. To know that the unexpressed spiritual desires are rooted in and are a measure of our spiritual maturity.

We have all had fights, but have you ever considered why we choose to fight? What causes us to fight?

Lesson Background

The Book of James was written to Jewish Christians in A.D. 49, by Jesus' brother, James. It serves as a life instruction guide for believers at all stages of maturity. Many compare it to the poetic book of Proverbs. We must be Christ-dependent in all our decisions and life priorities, and we must allow the Holy Spirit to season all our fomenting hearts' desires. As we confront differences of opinion, others' preferences, or divergent communication styles, these factors can lead to disagreements, even fights. The root of an erupted fight has a starting place that impacts every relationship we own, and that starting place is the focus of this lesson.

Read: James Chapters 1 and 4

Powerful Question: What is causing the quarrels and fights among you? Don't they come from the evil desires at war within you? (James 4:1 NLT)

Examining the Text

1. Verse 1 describes the place where fights with others begin. From where do they come?

_____

_____

_____

_____

_____

2. Name a few of the consequences that can result from a fight with another person. (Include verbal, physical or virtual fights.)

_____

_____

_____

_____

_____

3. How does James describe this inner issue that leads to fights with others? What can this mean? (1 Peter 2:11; Romans 7:14-15)

_____

_____

_____

_____

_____

4. How does Paul describe the change needed to overcome the carnal ways that lead us into conflicts? (Romans 12:2; 13:14; Proverbs 15:1-2)

5. For those who do not have what they desire after asking for it, James gives a reason why in verse 4. What is that reason? Explain.

6. Galatians 5:19-21 describes the unfruitful yields that come from a life rooted in a worldly, sinful nature. What are they?

7. In contrast to verses 19-21, Galatians 5:22 describes the yielded fruit that comes from a Holy Spirit-filled life. What are the "fruits of the spirit"?

---

8. If we find ourselves desiring to fight with others, what are some ways for us to contend with that spiritual issue? (Romans 12:10, 13, 15-16; 1 Peter 3:11; Philippians 2:3-4)

---

9. Is there a time when fighting is expected? (1 Timothy 6:12; 2 Timothy 4:7-8, 1 Peter 5:8-9, Ephesians 6:11-18, Romans 14:17-19)

Things to Remember

- We must be at peace within to be at peace with others.

- We must avoid coveting what others have.

- Worldly lusts and worldly thinking never bring satisfaction.

- Fights always have a reason rooted in some area of sin.

- The desires of our heart must be weighed against their benefit and practicality.

- It is possible to be at peace within when the Holy Spirit fills us (Ephesians 5:18).

- We must acknowledge that we have an internal war that only the Spirit can defeat.

- Man can't tame his inner battle alone.

- Sinful desires could stifle our ability to be fruitful for the kingdom, and they hinder our prayers.

Lesson Application

1. **If there is a desire to fight, I must consider what is causing that desire. What are some ways to get a spiritual victory that overcomes my desire to fight?**

2. **Make a daily list of blessings for which you are grateful.**

3. **Consider "why" you are asking for certain things in your prayer life. What would you do with it if you received it?**

Supporting Scriptures

- Proverbs 15:1-2 – A gentle answer deflects anger.

- Romans 7:14-15 – The trouble is not with the law. The trouble is with me. I'm a slave to sin.

- Romans 12:10 – Be transformed by the renewing of your mind, to prove the good and acceptable will of God.

- Romans 14:17-19 – Make every effort to do what leads to peace.

- Ephesians 6:11-18 – Put on the whole armor of God so that you will be able to stand.

- Ephesians 2:14-18. – God Himself is peace. He made peace, and He reconciled peace.
- Galatians 5:19 – If you follow the desires of your sinful nature, the results are very clear.
- Galatians 5:22 – The Holy Spirit produces this kind of fruit in our lives, including love and joy, and there is no law against such things.
- Philippians 2:3-4 – Do nothing out of vain, selfish ambition or conceit; value others above yourself.
- 1 Timothy 6:12 – Fight the good fight for the true faith.
- 1 Peter 2:11 – Keep away from worldly desires that wage war against your very souls.
- 1 Peter 3:11 – Turn away from evil and do good. Search for peace and work to maintain it.
- 2 Timothy 4:7-8 – I have fought the good fight; I have finished the race.
- 1 Peter 5:8-9 – The devil prowls around seeking whom he may devour.

UNIT I

REFLECTION AND APPLICATION

Aim

Use this session to share key discoveries made in the previous lessons. Review and discuss how the lessons have impacted you and how the lessons deepened your understanding of God's Word. Consider what changes the lessons have contributed to your spiritual growth. Most importantly, use this time to share how you have applied the lessons based upon what you have learned.

What were your take aways and life applications from these lessons?

Lesson 1 - My Brother's Keeper? (Genesis 4:9)

Lesson 2 - Limit on Forgiveness? (Matthew 18:21)

Lesson 3 - What About Leading Your Own? (1 Timothy 3:5)

Lesson 4 - What is Man? (Psalm 8:4)

Lesson 5 - Whom Will You Feed? (John 21:15-17)

Lesson 6 - The Start of Every Fight (James 4:1-2)

Powerful Questions in the Bible

*A Study of God's Voice Speaking
to His People*

UNIT II

MAN, WHERE ARE YOU?

Genesis 3:9

Lesson Aim:

To know that God pursues what He loves. To understand that God wants to have a whole relationship with us. To know that what we lose may have unintended consequences.

Lesson Background

This lesson focuses on Adam's story and the "original sin" committed in the Garden of Eden. Importantly, we look closely at the ramifications and consequences that accompany sin as we find that the unfolded Eden events are an archetype of what happens in a sin-marred relationship. Relationships are bonds, pledges held together with commonality and mutual interests, pursuing a shared destiny. A relationship's bond is stronger than the sum of the individuals alone. We can learn much about relationships from the Eden experience that can help us as we seek to nurture our respective relationships with Christ, family, friends, etc. Whole relationships are what God intended, and whole relationships are the substance upon which trust and prosperous growth can occur to produce healthy, abounding, and lasting bonds. Lastly, it is interesting to note that Genesis 3:9 is the first question attributed to God in the Bible.

Read: Genesis 2 and 3

Powerful Question: And the Lord God called unto Adam, and said unto him, "Where art thou?" (Genesis 3:9 KJV)

Answer: And he said, "I heard thy voice in the garden, and I was afraid, because I was naked; and I hid myself." (Genesis 3:10 KJV)

Examining the Text

1. From how many trees was Adam told that he could eat? (v. 2:16-17)

_____

_____

_____

_____

_____

2. If Adam and Eve ate from the Tree of the Knowledge of Good and Evil, what did the serpent promise them that was contrary to God's command? (v. 2:17)

_____

_____

_____

_____

_____

Consider: Had the other Garden of Eden trees become so familiar in taste, lacking in appeal, or poor in taste that Adam and Eve were enticed to try the one tree from which they were not permitted to eat? How does this situation resonate with us as we consider or are tempted to try or pursue what we do not have?

3. How are we also like Adam and Eve when it comes to the things that we have already
    been blessed with and our attraction to the things we do not have?

    _____

    _____

    _____

    _____

    _____

    _____

4. When God asked Adam, "Where are you?", could He have been seeking to know more
    than just Adam's physical location? Share your perspective.

    _____

    _____

    _____

    _____

    _____

    _____

5. What did Adam and Eve's sin lead them to do?

    _____

    _____

    _____

    _____

    _____

    _____

6. How do we know that God seeks a whole relationship with humanity? (Psalm 8:4-6; Acts 4:27; 1 John 3:1; Colossians 3:12; Deuteronomy 6:4-5)

_____

_____

_____

_____

_____

_____

_____

Consider: **Ways to measure the strength of our relationship with God**

   A. How much time have I spent in God's presence this week? Did I talk to Him daily?

   B. Does my life routine make God a priority?

   C. Am I actively engaged in what God desires for my life?

Colossians 3:17 *Do in word and deed, do all...*

7. Like Adam and Eve, what does it mean to have our eyes opened? (v. 7, James 1:14-16)

_____

_____

_____

_____

_____

_____

8. Beginning at Genesis 3:11, do we find the serpent speaking while God is confronting Adam about his sin, or after? Is this an observation to be noted when we are enticed by others?

9. What tools can we add to our daily living to fight against sinful enticements? (1 Peter 2:11; 1 Corinthians 6:18; 1 John 3:3; Joshua 1:8; Hebrews 4:16; 2 Corinthians 7:1)

10. Did Adam and Eve die when they ate the forbidden fruit?

Consider:

A. What are indications that a relationship with another person is healthy?

B. What are indications that a relationship with another person may be ruptured?

Things to Remember

- There was a relationship disruption between God and the created man, Adam.

- Healthy relationships and ruptured relationships both have signs that demonstrate their condition.

- The normal communication pattern between God and Adam had been altered by a poor choice and a destructive influence.

- We are prone to make poor choices when we do not believe we will be held account-able and when we take counsel from negative influences.

- God wants to know His relationship status with Adam—and with us.

- Hiding is not the way to deal with guilt.

- It is possible to sin so much that you sear your conscience; a natural sense of guilt for wrongs can be dulled (Ephesians 4:18-19).

- Adam told God that he became fearful because he was naked, not because he had sinned.

- God's question possibly rephrased: "I was expecting you to be where we normally meet. Why were you not there? Adam, are you lost or pre-occupied? I have come to find you." (We all need this type of concern for our wellbeing. We are lost without Jesus).

- God showed grace to Adam when he didn't deserve it due to his rebellion and sin. Adam, and all of us, deserve judgment, but God seeks to save us—even from ourselves.

Lesson Application

1. **In your prayer time, seek repentance for unconfessed sin and ask the Lord to reveal ways that you can strengthen your relationship with Him.**

2. **Make a list of your top three relationships. Then, list the ways that you can improve those relationships.**

Supporting Scriptures

- John 6:37 – Those the Father gives Me will come to me I will not reject them.
- Colossians 1:13-14 – For He has rescued us from the kingdom of darkness and transferred us into the Kingdom of His dear Son, who purchased our freedom and forgave our sins.
- Colossians 2:13-15 – You were dead because of your sins and because your sinful nature was not yet cut away. God made you alive with Christ; He forgave all our sins.
- Romans 6:11-12 – So you also should consider yourselves to be dead to the power of sin and alive to God through Christ Jesus. Do not let sin control the way you live…
- 2 Chronicles 19:9 – These were His instructions to them: "You must always act in the fear of the Lord, with faithfulness and an undivided heart."
- 1 John 2:24 – So you must remain faithful to what you have been taught.
- Psalm 8:4. What is man, that thou art mindful of him?

Next Lesson
"Get Off the Fence!"
1 Kings 18:21

GET OFF THE FENCE!

1 Kings 18:21

Lesson Aim:

To know a time will come when all must make a spiritual declaration. To know that God makes Himself real if we choose to see evidence of His presence. To know that a spiritually uncommitted life is a condemned life.

Lesson Background

The prophet Elijah declared a severe drought (17:1) that would last for three years. Now Elijah, who had been in hiding, sent word to King Ahab of Israel during the drought's third year that it would rain soon. Ahab had unsuccessfully searched all over trying to find Elijah. When Ahab meets Elijah, he calls him a troublemaker of Israel. Elijah tells Ahab to call together all the people of Israel, 450 of Baal's prophets, and 400 of Jezebel's prophets of Asherah to a meeting at Mt. Carmel. Boldly and publicly, Elijah challenges King Ahab, the Israelite people, and all the idol-worshipping prophets with a powerful question that forces everyone present to choose whom they will follow.

Powerful Question: Then Elijah stood in front of them and said, "How much longer will you waver, hobbling between two opinions? (1 Kings 18:21 NLT)

Answer: Complete silence. Elijah responds with a challenge that has Baal's prophets placing their sacrifice on their altar while Elijah places his sacrifice on a different altar.)

Examining the Text

1. Under what harsh environmental conditions were the people suffering? Why? (1 Kings 17:1)

_____

_____

_____

_____

_____

2. What kind of king was Ahab? (16:30, 33)

_____

_____

_____

_____

3. What does it mean to waver or hobble between differing opinions? (v. 21)

_____

_____

_____

_____

_____

For we are not fighting against flesh and blood enemies.

Ephesians 6:12 (NLT)

4. Name things or issues that can cause a person to stumble back and forth between the spiritual and carnal worlds.

    _____

    _____

    _____

    _____

    _____

5. When Elijah challenged the people with his question, what was their response? What could have been the reasons for their response? (v. 21)

    _____

    _____

    _____

    _____

    _____

6. When seeing God's awesome power on display compared to silence from the idol gods, despite the pagan priests' pleading all day for their gods to appear, how did the people respond then? (v. 39)

    _____

    _____

    _____

    _____

    _____

7. What personal idols might we have that may be affecting our spiritual growth?

_____

_____

_____

_____

_____

_____

Things to Remember

- It is highly possible that we will all have a Mount Carmel-like moment in our lives.
- How long will we function in indecision, operating below what God intended, living without fulfilling our God-given destiny or being controlled by worldly ways?
- The battle between spiritual and carnal is very real.
- We must be willing to lay down those things that have created separation between what we want and what God cherishes for us.
- God's people were asked to make a choice, yet they were silent when called to do so. We cannot, as believers, be silent nor make the expedient, carnal choice.
- God displays His superiority and power before His people, the false prophets, and to the idol worshippers.
- Sacrifice is required to remain spiritually obedient, strong, and faithful.

Lesson Application

1. **Our living witness is fortified in uncomfortable and fiery moments. Commit to praying for those who are enduring spiritual hardship and resistance because of their faith in Christ.**

2. **Pray that the Lord gives you spiritual discernment to refine your witness and dislodge any spiritual distractions aimed in your direction.**

Supporting Scriptures

- James 1:8 – A double-minded man is unstable in all his ways.
- Hosea 10:2 – Their heart is divided; now they shall be found faulty.
- Is. 29:13 – As much as this people draw near Me, their hearts are far from Me.
- I Corinthians 15:58 – Be steadfast, unmovable, always abounding in the work of the Lord.
- Romans 6:1 (NLT) – Well then, should we keep on sinning so that God can show us more and more of His wonderful grace?
- Joshua 24:15 – Choose today whom you will serve; as for me and my house, we will serve the Lord
- 2 Kings 17:14-15, 20; Zephaniah 1:5-6; 1 Kings 19:10, 14 – Idol worship and spiritual decay.

Additional Background information

- Elijah repaired the broken altar for his sacrifice (v. 30).
- He used twelve stones to rebuild the altar, each representing an Israel/Judah tribe.
- Elijah fully water-saturated his sacrifice, the altar, and the wood beneath it.
- Elijah called on God and fire from heaven fell and consumed his stone altar, the wood, the dust, the water around the altar, and the sacrifice.
- The people fell on their faces, crying out, "The Lord—He is God! Yes, the Lord is God!"
- Elijah ordered that all of Baal's prophets be killed, and they were.
- Elijah ordered Ahab to go back to Jezreel because a mighty rainstorm was coming, and the rain fell as prophesied.
- Elijah outran a chariot to get back to Jezreel ahead of the King.

Next Lesson
"Lord, Where Are You"
Matthew 2:2

LORD, WHERE ARE YOU?

Matthew 2:2

Aim:

To know that God pursues what He loves. To understand that God sent His very best. To know there is value and a reward for those who sincerely pursue Him.

Lesson Background

There are replete examples surrounding Christ's birth that demonstrate how we can pursue and get to know Him as the true and living Savior. His birth had been foretold for generations and there was great anticipation for the Messiah's arrival. This portion of the Christ Child's arrival focuses on how His birth attracted onlookers. The radiant star in the sky, signifying Christ's birth, was so evident that men from faraway lands were drawn to the star's symbolic, messianic fulfillment. Our lesson is the first question recorded in the New Testament, and it is emblematic of humankind's pursuit of God. In our previous study lesson from Genesis 2, "Man, Where Art Thou?," we noted the reverse: God is pursuing man. Now, it is mankind, the Magi, from far eastern lands, seeking God's Son. The Magi first visited Judea's King Herod to inquire about the newborn King of the Jews. Eventually, their journey takes them to their desired destination to worship the true King and Messiah.

Powerful Question: "Where is He that is born of the Jews?" Matthew 2:2

Answer: In Bethlehem of Judea, for so it is written by the prophet. This was the answer given to King Herod by his leading priests and teachers of religious law, when he inquired about where the Messiah would be born Matthew 2:5.

Examining the Text

1. What did the Magi seek to do when they arrived in Jerusalem and appeared before King Herod? (v. 2)

2. How did King Herod react to these strangers' (the Magi's) request? (v. 3)

3. Having concerns about the reported newborn King, Jesus, whom did Herod send to investigate the issue, and what might this say about Herod's leadership? (vv. 7-8)

4. When the Magi saw the Christ Child, what two key actions did they perform that we are to consistently replicate in our spiritual lives? (v. 11)

_____

_____

_____

_____

_____

_____

Questions we can ask ourselves as we ponder the Magi's pursuit of worship
- How far are we willing to go for a worship experience?
- What are we willing to leave behind to have an encounter with God?
- What are we willing to bring to the worship experience?

5. When it was time to leave, what did the Magi do? Why? What can we learn from their example? (v. 12)

_____

_____

_____

_____

_____

_____

_____

6. How much effort do we really put into pursuing God?

_____

_____

_____

_____

_____

_____

7. Are we tempted to give up when our respective journeys are not what we expected? Explain.

_____

_____

_____

_____

_____

_____

Can you name the Wisemen's (Magi's) gifts?

- _____, a suitable gift for a king
- _____, a gift for a deity
- _____, smoky fragranced spice for someone who is going to die

(Note: The gifts are believed to be the financial resources needed for Jesus's family's travel to Egypt.)

8. What would be examples or evidence that we are choosing to pursue God in our lives? (Jeremiah 29:13-14; John 14:21)

_____

_____

_____

_____

_____

_____

9. Provide illustrations of behaviors and actions that demonstrate that man is pursuing the interests of man. (E.g., greed)

_____

_____

_____

_____

_____

_____

Lesson Application

1. **Knowing that God rewards those who diligently seek Him, memorize three scriptures found in this lesson.**

2. **Make plans to give away one treasured or meaningful item to someone who is not expecting it.**

Supporting Scriptures

- Numbers 24:17 – Balaam speaks of a star rising out of Jacob.

- 1 Chronicles 16:11 – Seek the Lord and His strength; seek His presence continually!

- Proverbs 8:17 – I love those who love Me, and those who seek Me diligently find Me.

- Isaiah 55:6-7 – Seek the Lord while He may be found.

- Jeremiah 23:5 – The days are coming, declares the Lord, when I will raise up for David a righteous Branch, a King who will reign wisely and do what is just and right in the land.

- Hosea 10:12 – It is the time to seek the Lord that He may come and rain righteousness upon you.

- Micah 5:2 – Messiah would be born in Bethlehem.

- Luke 2:4 – David was in Bethlehem, his ancient home from Nazareth in Galilee, because he was a descendant of King David.

- Luke 11:9-10 – Ask, seek and you will find, knock and the door will be opened.

- Luke 12:29-31; Matthew 6:33 – But seek first His kingdom and His righteousness.

- John 14:21 – Obey the commands to show love for Christ, and the Father will love them, too.

- Acts 17:21 – We should seek God, perhaps feel our way toward Him, and find Him. Yet, He is not far from each of us.

- Hebrews 11:6 – He rewards those who seek Him.

The James 4:8 and 10 Spiritual Pursuit Checkup

- Draw close to God – open your heart, listen to His voice, and then follow His plan
- Cleanse yourself – remove and cease holding onto any spiritually tainting ways
- Purify your heart – seek and pursue truth, sincerity, and transparency
- Walk with humility in all the places where God leads you to be

Notes on Herod

- Half Jewish; he ruled 33 years (37 B.C. to 4 B.C.) during the Roman reign of Antony and Augustus.

- Had several children; had at least one wife killed.

- Was not the rightful heir to David's throne.

- Was hated by the Jews as a usurper.

- Was a ruthless king with many enemies.

- Did not want the Jews to unite around a religious king of a religious people.

- Knew that the people were anticipating a Messiah's arrival (Luke 3:15).

- Ordered all babies under age two to be murdered (2:16); sought to murder Christ.

- Died from an incurable disease.

- Kingdom was divided among his three sons: Herod Antipas, Archelaus, Herod Philip II.

Next Lesson
"Is there Anything He Cannot Do?"
Matthew 8:27

"IS THERE ANYTHING GOD CANNOT DO?"

Matthew 8:27

Aim

To know that the power of Christ is a constant hedge of protection around us. To know that the power of Christ is neither dictated to nor limited by any other. To know that the inerrant power of Christ is displayed how and when He chooses.

Background

Jesus had preached the "Sermon on the Mount" (Matthew 5-7), and the crowds were so excited. They had never heard anyone speak with such authority, wisdom, and conviction. The enthralled crowd wanted more, so they followed Him as He came down from the mountain. He then performed several miracles before deciding to leave the area by boat. Jesus and His disciples were crossing the Sea of Galilee when a violent storm arose while He slept in the lower part of the boat. His disciples gallantly fought the raging waves crashing over the top of the boat, but the storm was too great and their efforts were futile. They believed they would not survive.

Powerful Question: And the men marveled, saying, "What sort of man is this, that even the winds and the sea obey Him?" (Matthew 8:27 ESV; cf. Mark 4:35-41; Luke 8:22-25)

Answer: His disciples were without words to describe what had just happened.

Examining the Text

1. Has there been a time when an event or situation occurred that was simply beyond words?

2. Before the miracle, what was the disciples' greatest concern? (v. 25)

3. What was Jesus' greatest concern for His disciples? (v. 26)

> *"Do not be afraid" appears 365 times in the Bible. Once for each day of the year.*

4. When asking what manner or type of man Jesus was, were they questioning His background, the extent of His power, the source of His power, or something else?

_____

_____

_____

_____

_____

5. Describe something you have experienced or seen that seemed to defy reality or human capability?

_____

_____

_____

_____

_____

6. What manner of God do we serve? Describe Him by what He has done or is doing for you.

_____

_____

_____

_____

_____

7. What life questions are you facing that only an all-powerful, all-loving God can handle?

_____

_____

_____

_____

_____

_____

8. How do our actions demonstrate our knowledge of Christ's power over whatever challenges we are facing?

_____

_____

_____

_____

_____

_____

Things to Remember

- Jesus follows up a mighty message with might acts.
- Jesus was more concerned about their spiritual maturity than their physical dilemma.
- When Jesus moves, all elements, spaces, people, and time are brought under subjection to Him.
- Besides trusting, the disciples did all they knew to do to deal with the violent storm, but to no avail.
- By His mere spoken word, the storm was vanquished.
- Life does not always provide answers to the who, what, when, where, why, or how regarding the things that happen in our lives.

> ### *Faith and Fear*
> ### *Faith is Forwarding All Issues To Heaven; Forsaking All, I Trust Him*
> ### *Fear is False Evidence Appearing Real*

Life Application

1. **To love Christ is to obey Him and trust Him. As you consider your burdens, speak aloud in the mirror each morning, "Lord, I trust You today!"**

2. **During your time of meditation and prayer, recall what He has done for you in the past, how He has made a way and provided. Thank Him and praise Him that what you are facing is just another battle already won.**

Supporting Scriptures

- Psalm 56:3 – When I am afraid, I will trust in You.
- Proverbs 30:5 – Every word of God is true; He is a shield.
- Isiah 41:10 – So don't fear, I am with you.
- Romans 5:3 – Tribulation works patience.
- Romans 8:38 – Nothing can separate us from God's love that is in Christ Jesus.
- Romans 10:17 – Faith comes by hearing and hearing by the Word of God.
- Philippians 1:21 – To live is Christ and to die is gain.
- Philippians 4:11 – I've learned to be content whatsoever state I am in.
- Hebrews 11:1 – Faith is the substance of things hoped for, the evidence of things not seen.
- 1 John 4:18 – Love drives out fear.

> ### Next Lesson
> ### "It's Not What They Call You"
> ### Matthew 16:13

IT'S NOT WHAT THEY CALL YOU

Matthew 16:13

★ ★ ★

Lesson Aim

To know that what Jesus means to us is influenced by how we experience Him. To know that we can have more than one relationship with Jesus. To share our testimony based on how we have experienced Him.

Lesson Background

Jesus' earthly ministry seemed dormant for nearly 20 years, but then He took to the streets with miracles and a profound Word. His ministry was unlike anything in the history of the world. He drew thousands and saved many. In his crowds were true believers, casual observers, critics, religious leaders, conspirators seeking to silence Him, users, the wealthy, and the broken. In Matthew 16, His acclaim was on the rise, the demands on His time were non-stop, and He had to be on guard against His opposers. To keep His pace and His purpose, He occasionally stole away from the crowds to recharge and connect with God the Father. The focus of this study centers on how Jesus is defined and considered. As He ministered, there was ongoing confusion and curiosity about what Jesus should be called? Who was this man?

Powerful Question: When Jesus came to the region of Caesarea Philippi, He asked His disciples, "Who do people say that the Son of Man is?" Matthew 16:13 (NLT)

"It ain't what they call you, it's what you answer to." – W.C. Fields

Answer:

Examining the Text

1. What did Jesus ask His disciples privately in verse 13? What were their responses?

   _____

   _____

   _____

   _____

   _____

   _____

   _____

   _____

2. Describe and explain the difference between what Jesus asked them in verse 13 and what He asked in verse 15.

   _____

   _____

   _____

   _____

   _____

   _____

   _____

   _____

   _____

> *"I am the way, truth and the life."*
>
> *John 14:6 (NLT)*

3. How likely is it that we may be called something different based on an experience someone has had with us? Explain. Provide examples of ways that we may be identified by others who know us.

_____

_____

_____

_____

_____

_____

4. Who responded to Jesus's question in verse 15, and what did he say? From your perspective, how did the one who responded come to his conclusion?

_____

_____

_____

_____

_____

_____

5. Let's reimagine the question in verse 13 and reshape it as if we are asking it to others around us. What would we ask?

_____

_____

_____

_____

6. How does our experience with Jesus impact the way we serve Him, respond to Him, and seek to please Him?

_____

_____

_____

_____

_____

_____

_____

7. What is the difference between who you believed Jesus to be earlier in your Christian walk and who He is now?

_____

_____

_____

_____

_____

_____

_____

8. Why do you praise Him and how? Why do you believe in Him and how? Why is He a priority and how? Why are you determined to serve Him and how? Because He is...

_____

_____

_____

_____

_____

_____

9. What were Jesus's instructions to His disciples in verse 20?

_____

_____

_____

_____

_____

_____

_____

Lesson Application

1. **Make a list of all that God is to you.**
2. **Pray that God will make Himself an abiding presence in your life, to season your words with discernment and Godly love.**

Supporting Scriptures

- Malachi 4:5 – Sending the prophet Elijah before the dreadful day of the Lord arrives.
- John 6:69 – We know You are the Holy One of God.
- John 11:27 – I have always believed You are the Messiah, Son of God.
- Galatians 1:16 – To reveal His Son to me so that I would proclaim.
- John 1:42 – Your name is Simon, but you will be called Cephas.
- 1 Corinthians 3:11 – No one can lay a foundation other than the one.
- Ephesians 2:20-22 – The cornerstone is Christ Jesus Himself.
- Ephesians 4:15-16 – Christ, who is the head of His body, the church.
- 1 Peter 2:4-5 – Christ, who is the living cornerstone, chosen by God for great honor.

Those Who Experienced Him During His Earthly Ministry Called Him:

- Healer
- Great Teacher
- Miracle Worker
- Forgiver
- Prophet
- …and more

The Pharisees and Sadducees called Him (from the Gospel of John):

- Non-keeper of the Sabbath and a sinner (disobedient) (7:16)
- An illegitimate child born of fornication (8:41)
- A Samaritan (mixed-blood outsider) with a demon (8:48, 52)
- Blasphemer: a phony law-breaker who disrespected God who made Himself a God (10:33)
- A mere man whose signs are mere magic tricks (11:47)
- Potential political establishment disrupter and rabble rouser (11:48)

Do you know who He is to you?

Then…

Believe it fully,

Live it fully,

Testify about it boldly!

UNIT II, LESSON 6

REFLECTION AND APPLICATION

Aim

Use this session to share key discoveries made in the previous lessons. Review and discuss how the lessons have impacted you and how the lessons deepened your understanding of the Word. Consider what changes the lessons have made in your spiritual growth. Most importantly, use this time to share how you have applied the lessons based on what you have learned.

What were your takeaways and life applications from these lessons?

Lesson 1 - Man, Where Are You? (Genesis 3:9)

Lesson 2 - Get Off The Fence! (1 Kings 18:21)

Lesson 3 - Lord, Where Are You? (Matthew 2:2)

Lesson 4 - Is There Anything God Cannot Do? (Matthew 8:27)

Lesson 5 - It's Not What They Call You (Matthew 16:13)

Powerful Questions in the Bible

A Study of God's Voice Speaking to His People

APPENDIX

FACILITATOR'S INSTRUCTION GUIDE

★ ★ ★

Bountiful blessings! I am greatly encouraged that you will be sharing these important, biblical **Powerful Questions** with students of the Gospel. As these lessons were given to me, I was enlightened and inspired to make this study useful at all levels of the Christian walk.

Whether your learning time will be in-person or via a virtual platform, and whether it will be within a small group or a large student setting, you will be well-equipped and blessed by a learning experience like no other. Allow yourself to be transparent and Holy Spirit-led, but also silent where Scripture is silent. Each lesson is meant to be an introspective probe and journey through the **Powerful Questions**, to identify with the characters in each lesson while finding your own answers as the **Powerful Questions** resonate with your personal experiences.

The facilitator serves as a guide through the learning experience, a spotlight captain, and a timekeeper to ensure the study remains on schedule. Know that the Spirit will empower you, but also allow yourself ample time to be fully prepared for the experience using the Facilitator's instructions provided below.

Personal Preparation

A. Send advance announcements promoting the experience.
B. Pray at the start of your study time, that you will receive discernment and clarity. Be encouraged in your preparation.
C. Read all materials, questions, answers, supporting verses, and at least the previous and succeeding chapters. Use commentaries or translations that will aide your quest

for a deeper, shared learning experience rooted in a contextual understanding of the text.

D. Focus on **why** the text was given, **who** the intended audience is, **what** the circumstance are that surround the Scripture, and how it can be applied to your and your participants' lives.

E. As for lesson pace, each *lesson does not have to be completed in one session.* The material is robust and one lesson may require multiple sessions to complete. Measure each session's pace and note opportunities to lean in on a topic when depth may be required, while also ensuring consistent forward movement towards completion.

F. Have a set agenda that includes a time schedule for each part of the class. An agenda suggestion is provided below for a one hour and thirty minute class. Use the class time wisely, leaving at least ten minutes towards the end of the session for application and reflection.

G. As you travel to class, pray for the Lord's Word to come forth.

H. Ensure each student has the class materials in advance, no less than two weeks prior. The material encourages participants to do prior study and mediation, to optimize each lesson's learning and sharing experience.

I. Arrive early to greet each student as they enter the class.

J. Use an attendance sheet or electronic log for each session.

K. For in-person classes, provide writing instruments for the students, if needed.

L. Conclude each session with time for you to summarize what was covered in the lesson and mention the study text for the next session.

Class Start

A. Begin class on time with a warm welcome. Introduce yourself, if necessary.

B. Facilitate a brief ice breaker (e.g. an illustration, tasteful joke, or a student recognition).

C. Open with prayer. Designate a participant, letting them know in advance.

Launching into the Lesson

A. Share the class lesson title and scripture text.

B. Read the **Lesson Aim** (either you or a participant.)

C. Select a student to read the Lesson Background.

D. Read the Powerful Question and Powerful Answer text.

E. Read each question in the Examining the Text and listen for key points to re-emphasize or delve into for further, deeper discussion.

F. Students are instructed to identify and then circle/highlight the Examining the Text questions that speak powerfully to something they have personally experienced or are experiencing in their walk with God and others. Ask students to share those responses.

G. Personal stories or examples are excellent, but be careful not to over-talk the lesson. This is a shared discussion and a group learning experience.

H. Encourage class dialogue that gives all who are comfortable with sharing their insights a chance to do so. However, the time should not be dominated by one or two voices. Know how to tactfully keep the discussion moving to ensure completion of the lesson.

I. Fold in supporting scriptures that align with each question. Watch your time.

J. You may be unable to fully discuss each question if you attempt to cover each lesson in one session.

K. It is ok if you choose to spend additional sessions on areas of emphasis, but still move the class through the content while remaining focused on the Lesson Aim.

L. After the questions, optionally, read through the **Key Themes** learned.

Concluding the Lesson

A. Conclude each lesson with the **Lesson Application** and a reflective discussion on what was learned. We suggest 10 minutes for this discussion.

B. Ask if there are any prayer requests or announcements.

C. In the closing prayer, lift elements from what was shared in the session and the prayer requests, and also pray for each student's continued spiritual growth.

D. End at the specified time. Encourage students to prepare for the next week's lesson as early as possible for effective learning, personal growth, and discussion.

E. Track the number of attendees and note new attendees.

Reflection Week

A. This is an important part of the learning experience. It creates spiritual connection among the students. Use session time to revisit and reignite key learnings, personal insights, and study applications.

B. Recognize students who participated in all the lessons.

C. Use the attendance sheet to send emails to students about future study opportunities.

Session Agenda (suggested)

6:00	Welcome, self-introduction, and prayer
6:05	Lesson Aim
6:07	Lesson Background and Powerful Question and Answer scriptures
6:15	Examine the Text questions
7:10	Key Themes and background scriptures
7:15	Lesson Application
7:25	Closing announcements and prayer
7:30	Dismissal

Please be sensitive to students who want to share personal matters after class has concluded.

Sample Ice Breaker

The football coach was about to give one of his famous locker room pep talks when he looked at his star defensive linebacker and asked him to say the Lord's Prayer at the end. The star quarterback snickered to his wide receiver, "I'll bet you $50 he doesn't know the Lord's Prayer." After the coach finished, the linebacker began, "Now I lay me down to sleep, I pray the Lord my soul to keep…" The quarterback tapped the wide receiver on the shoulder, handed him $50 and said, "I had no idea he knew the Lord's Prayer."

Powerful Questions in the Bible

A Study of God's Voice Speaking to His People

LESSON
ANSWER KEYS

Preparation and Use

Important: Answer Key responses have been researched and cross-referenced, but note that some answers are opinions solely of the author. Use these answers in your study and reference them while facilitating. The Answer Key content is substantially more than can be shared in any single session, but the answers and accompanying Scripture references will provide insight and aid you with topical flow.

Unit I, Lesson 1
Answer Key
"My Brother's Keeper?"
Genesis 4:9

Examining the Text

1. **What act of worship were Cain and Abel expected to perform? Was there a difference in how the two men carried out their requirement? (vv. 3-5)**

   - Giving an offering back to God from what He had provided.

   - God had arranged a pre-determined time and manner for them to give their offerings. Their offerings were not expected to be the same, but the protocol and attitudes were.

   - Abel gave from the best of his livestock in the right portions. Cain, as a farmer, gave a portion from his harvest, but it is questionable whether what he gave was the right amount or the right items. Both men predetermined what they were going to give.

   - A choice to give less or inferior items is far below God's standard, whether giving to Him or to others.

   - The gifts each were given were to be a representation of gratitude, thanks, and trust.

   - Even if Cain gave the right-sized offering, it would still be rejected. His attitude or timing did not meet the required standard.

   - Our gifts to God are filtered through His eyes.

2. **What can we understand about God's instruction and tone by how He responded to Cain's offering? (vv. 6-7)**

- God was empathetic. He instructed Cain on how to improve; He wanted to help him.

- God gave Cain a warning about the correlation between sin and his poor attitude.

- God insisted to Cain that he can have power over sin.

- God tried to console Cain in his despondence after He confronted him about his offering.

- God was sorrowful, but not dismissive.

- God was encouraging. He urged that Cain could meet the standard with an improved attitude.

- God was instructional. He wanted to help Cain get up to standard while reinforcing the giving standard.

- God was forgiving. He wanted to give Cain another chance to correct his attitude.

- God was firm. He has a standard that does not change because someone does not follow it—a standard that was made clear to both Cain and Abel.

Do all things without grumbling or disputing. Philippians 2:14 (ESV)

3. **What was Cain's response when God told him his offering was inadequate? (v. 5; 1 Samuel 16:7; Luke 22:31)**

- Cain was angered and his countenance became glum.

- Cain was embarrassed and hurt for the wrong reasons. He was hurt because of God's response and not because of his own actions, which is blame transference. He was unwilling to be accountable and remorseful for the proper reasons.

- Cain's attitude when giving his offering was not what was expected.

- Cain's intent behind his offering was not in line with the proper reverence for God's standard.

- If a man will disrespect God, then what will he do to a fellow man?

- Cain also likely looked over at Abel's offering in jealousy, envy, and anger. Sin in one's heart becomes an act, a pattern, a lifestyle of destructive actions.

4. Was it Cain's perception that God had rejected him, his offering, or both?

- Cain's ego told him that God rejected him.

- The substandard offering was merely a side issue for what Cain believed was a personal attack on his worthiness.

- It is an error for us to base our identity of who we are on what we do for a living, the relationships we hold, or any accomplishments we have achieved.

5. What can we learn from Abel and the sacrifice he chose to give God? (v. 4; Luke 6:38)

- Abel's offering was given according to God's instruction. By God's reaction, some would argue that he exceeded God's standard.

- Abel's offering was given the right way, with the right motivation based on the instructions that had been previously given. He desired and cherished having a right relationship with God, starting with obedience.

- Abel's offering was given in faith, not knowing if God would provide more.

- God was pleased with Abel's offering and viewed it with favor, delight.

- Have you ever received a gift from someone and when they gave it to you, it was nice but their attitude about giving it was off? What impact does that have on your thoughts about the gift and about that person?

- Abel brought the fatty portions—the largest and most healthy portions—from some of the first born from his livestock. Everything he gave was fresh and bountiful, because that is how he felt about God.

- We should give and receive more than we can grasp or conceive.

- We, too, please God when we give our best.

6. In this lesson, we see that God confronted Cain in his sin. What should be our Godly response if confronted with our sin? (Psalm 139:23-24; 2 Samuel 12:13; 1 John 1:8-9; 2 Corinthians 7:9-10)

- Humility, to ask God to search our heart for impurity.

- Confession, as David did when confronted by Nathan

- Acknowledgement of the sin, asking for forgiveness.

- Heartfelt commitment to turn away from sin; repentance.

- Reliance on a trustworthy Christian to support and guide us during uncertain life issues.

- Acceptance of forgiveness.

- Removal of influences that caused the sin.

- Reparation for anyone who was injured by our sin(s). Well-known examples to follow include David by Nathan, Jonah, Saul/Paul on the road to Damascus

Discussion Spotlight: How many of us want special consideration when our situation, attitude, or performance does not meet an agreed expectation level?

- Are we accountable when we fail to meet an expected standard?

- Can we accept the consequences that may accompany an attitude or production failure?

7. How did Cain express his anger toward God, and where did he commit his deed? Is the place where he committed his fatal sin significant? (v. 6-8; 1 John 3:12)

- Cain killed his brother. Some contend that when a murderer puts their hands on the victim, it is a sign of a higher degree of rage.

- Cain's anger was violent, raging.

- Cain showed displaced aggression.

- Cain slew Abel in the fields—the very place where God brings life up from the ground, the place where Cain drew life-giving sustenance, the place from where he was to draw a good offering, his place of work where he applied his life skill.

8. How serious, as God confronted Cain, was the blood on the ground? (Leviticus 17:10-14)

- Abel's blood and life fluids were crying out in agony to God, Abel's Creator.

- Blood is associated with the life in any creature.

- Blood is used for atonement, cleansing in a worshipful, symbolic context.

9. **When God, in verse 9, inquired about what Cain had done, what was Cain's response? What was Cain effectively saying in his response to God?**

    - "Am I my brother's keeper?"

    - Cain's response is the first recorded act of verbal insolence toward God.

    - Why should I care? He is not my concern.

    - Are you adding to my responsibilities, now?

    - You go find him, I'm not.

    - Abel is a grown man with his own life, and I have my own life.

    - So, again, you are more concerned about him than me?

10. **What does it mean to be our brother's or sister's keeper? In what ways can we demonstrate love for others?**

    - We can be thoughtful about their welfare.

    - We should not seek their harm in word or deed, but rather their good.

    - We can be kind, gentle, and loving.

    - We can be watchful over them.

    - Love, protection, care, and concern are all part of "keeping" our brother or sister.

11. **What more do we learn in verse 13 about Cain's heart**

    - Cain was not remorseful nor accountable; he was self-centered.

    - Cain was showing great hardness of heart to be more concerned about his sufferings than his sins.

    - Cain valued a close relationship with God after it was much too late.

    - Cain was a fearful man and a dangerous man.

    - Cain was a marked man for life.

Unit I, Lesson 2
Answer Key
"Limit on Forgiveness?"
Matthew 18:21

Discussion Spotlight: Have any of the following incidents happened to you? (Royce)

- *Something of value being stolen from you? (For me, it was a large rabbit piggy bank, a boombox from my car, a vanity license plate, and money.)*

- *Someone intentionally attempting to cause you physical, financial, or emotional harm? (For me, it was someone who lied to a supervisor about me because of jealousy. Another person spread untrue rumors about me after I would not let him control me with his ideas of how to handle issues. One person had flyers made and distributed that misrepresented me. Then there was the person who posted on social media and mailed poorly written attacks to my home. Someone else spread lies to that person and a close relative, because I disagreed with certain deceptions.)*

Examining the Text

1. **If we look closely at Peter's question in verse 21, what was he asking Jesus?**

   - Should I stop forgiving people who repeatedly offend?

   - At what point does revenge or dismissal enter the equation when someone offends repeatedly?

   - Could you provide a set standard or rule to know when you have done all you can in a relationship that has been serially damaged by sin lapses?

   - Is there a point when a person or a relationship is no longer worth salvaging?

   - Should a believer continue a relationship that is serially compromised by the deeds of another?

2. **In Peter's question, what was likely his greatest concern? was it the seriousness of an act against him, the number of times an act had been committed, or the way he should respond to an offending party? Further, what should we be most concerned about when we are wronged by another person? (vv. 21 and 15)**

   - Peter wanted to know the point at which a person is deemed incapable of receiving forgiveness.

   - Peter believed a person cannot be serious about a relationship based on some set number of misdeeds.

   - At what point, Peter's question implied, do you quit trying and give up on a person? When is enough *enough*? How long must one endure the fallout, the hits, and the damage from a repeat offender?

   - Just as Jesus forgives all sins, sin is still sin, and there is no reason to track the number of repeat incidents.

   - Peter seemed to imply that when offenses reach a certain point, no more forgiveness can or should be extended for future offenses.

   - He looked for clarification to determine whether preserving a relationship is worth it when there are repeated sins or offending incidents.

   - Must there be a way to measure if what the offending person has done is intentional? Should the extent of the damage be considered?

   - Peter may not have agreed with the viable possibility that spiritual strength and wisdom can come from mistakes.

   - Peter's position seemed to miss the fact that a limit cannot impact an offender's actual sincerity.

   - Should I track the wrongs against me so that I will know when the pre-determined offense limit has been reached?

3. **Was Peter's thinking counter to Christ's teachings and, if so, how? (v. 22l 6:14-15; 5:7)**

   - Yes, the limit is counter to Christ's teachings, as He gave a hypothetical calculation that no one would dare try to track. The lesson cautions that we need to know when we may be on the other side of the sin table seeking forgiveness, too.

- Peter was operating under the law and not under eternal grace.

Jewish Law on Forgiveness - *teshuvah*

4. **What assurance or guarantees come with forgiving someone? Share your thoughts or concerns about extending forgiveness?**
   - Forgiveness *comes with no guarantees*. I may be wronged again, for the same reason by the same person.
   - Forgiveness is a trust walk that the offender will accept accountability, seek to make retribution, and take the steps to understand why they did what they did and whom they impacted. Their offense could cost me resources or reputation.
   - The offender may not be sincere. They may be buying more time to do something else. They could be a user who sees me as a naive stool pigeon. Plus, just amends may not be extended to me when I need it.
   - Forgiveness *does not require that we wait for a person to behave a certain way* to meet our approval. (Don't let the sun go down on your wrath. Be kind, tenderhearted…)

5. **When Jesus gave an equation to determine how many times to extend forgiveness (see KJV v. 22),** should Peter or we take this number literally?
   - Four hundred and ninety (490) is an absurd number that demonstrates the absurdity of setting an arbitrary limit for forgiving a repeat offender.
   - Christ wants forgiveness to be extended without a tally board.
   - When we consider how often we have sinned in God's presence, we have all probably exceeded whatever maximum number of times it has happened. Not to mention that we may show no inclination to take proper accountability nor make sufficient retribution.

- Do we actually keep count of the number of times someone has wronged us?
- Jesus challenges the disciples to reply with a negotiated number lower than His.

6. **What essential elements are included in forgiveness? (See Genesis 50:17-21)**
   - The offender seeks it.
   - The offender's contrition.
   - Our consideration for the person seeking forgiveness, imagining being on the other side.
   - Our tender, loving response to the one seeking forgiveness.
   - Our letting go of the hurt.
   - Marking a new beginning.
   - Our recognizing that when we forgive, we too receive forgiveness. (Matthew 6:14-15)
   - Prayer for the person who hurt us.

7. **How does forgiveness affect our prayer life? (Mark 11:25; Matthew 5:23-24)**
   - Forgive others first and then we receive the Father's forgiveness.
   - We are not to seek His presence or give Him gifts without first reconciling with a brother in Christ.
   - Each of us has benefitted from an untold number of generous acts of forgiveness, and Christ continues to forgive.
   - Christ's ultimate sacrifice was all about the forgiveness we needed, that could not be remedied any other way.

8. **What will result from the forgiveness we extend? (Matthew 6:14; Luke 6:37-38; Genesis 50:20-21)**
   - The Father will forgive us our sins.
   - It starts by asking us to not be so hard on others. Eliminate judgmental and condemning dispositions so that we can be clearly focused on repairing sin's broken relationships.

- Forgiving may be the path to both self-renewal and newness for the one who needs to be forgiven.

- When someone wrongs us, it may not be intentional. We may have perceived things in error, we may have been unaware of the full circumstances, or the offender may have a different comfort and expression level in the relationship.

- Forgiving is giving to another what returns in overflow and abundance right back to us at the same level of measured generosity. There's a bountiful blessing in our forgiveness.

- Forgiveness means that I no longer charge another's error as an unpaid debt, a clean slate.

- Forgiveness means that the one who is wronged takes the next proactive step in the relationship. Timing is important, and so is the attitude.

- Carrying a list of wrongs done to us is a burden to us.

- See Genesis 50:20-21 when Joseph chose to not take vengeance against his brothers.

9. **On what basis do I have the option to write someone off with no possibility of forgiveness? (Romans 12:1-3; Mark 8:34-35)**

- None, unless we are living and working by the dying world's standards.

- Our bodies are to be offered in a spiritual way as sacrifices that demonstrate our worship of Christ. We carry out this sacrifice in ways, not according to the world but that are life transforming in thought and action. Such spiritual sacrifice requires a commitment to humility and to clear thought.

- Placing ourselves in a position to extend forgiveness nullifies the world's damaging and distracting forgiveness patterns.

- We need to get rid of things that diminish our capacity to function daily at our spiritual peak. We can reshape our routines to better discern the voice of God and the daily direction He has set for us. In contrast, the pagan pursuit of pleasure and worldly affirmations are useless).

- Each of our journeys is different.

10. **What can we learn and apply from verses 15-17 that will help us extend forgiveness?**

   - These verses provide a process by which we bring a fault or sin committed against us to the offending party.

   - Start with a one-on-one discussion about the wrong. Bringing others too early into the issue changes the dynamic from a one-on-one exchange to what may seem like a one-against-several type of ambush.

   - If unresolved, try again by bringing one or two others as witnesses (not as the primary mouthpiece).

   - If still unresolved, bring the matter before the church (or its leadership).

   - If no resolution after going through the process, then treat the person as a pagan or a tax collector. Tax collectors were disliked because they often collected more than was required so that they could pad their own pockets. They were fraudulent tricksters who took advantage of the poor and the weak.

11. **Again, why must I forgive?**

   - We ourselves have been given so many chances and new starts. Many of those restarts are unmerited.

   - So, the application of forgiveness is not what we can do for our offenders, but it is a recognition of what we can do for ourselves, our own heart.

> **Unit I, Lesson 3**
> **Answer Key**
> **"What About Leading Your Own?"**
> **1 Timothy 3:5**

Examining the Text

1. **Those desiring to be church leaders should know that church work is good work, but there are requirements. The first requirement is outlined in verse 2. What is it and what does it mean? (Titus 1:7-8; Acts 20:28; 1 Timothy 4:12)**

   - Church leaders are to be blameless.

   - Church leaders are to live a life that is clean of immorality and unrepentant sin.

   - Church leadership calls for a standard that will be emulated by those whom the pastor leads.

   - Church leadership qualification requirements do not include popularity, ability to sing, or personal relationships.

   - The disciplined life of a church leader requires commitment, great effort, and intention.

   - The standard of being blameless also applies for all believers.

   - A qualified church leader is not arrogant, quick-tempered, a heavy drinker, violent, or dishonest with money.

2. **Is the blameless standard too high of a bar for anyone? How can it be reached? (2 Corinthians 13:11, 2 Peter 1:5-8)**

   - Yes, the standard is high, as it should be. Is it achievable? A qualified church leader will strive to meet up to it.

   - Church leaders have been given a great responsibility to carry God's Word in action.

   - Spiritual maturity is a process, and that is why selecting qualified leaders in the local church body should be handled with care.

- Faith and belief alone are not enough to be a leader. These must be accompanied by moral excellence, self-control, and more.

3. **Verse 2 speaks of leader qualifications that include temperance, sober minded-ness, and good behavior. How do these qualifications impact a church's effort to create one-mindedness?**

- These qualifications keep the church from placing leaders who are divisive or non-responsive.
- Qualified leaders seek to make sound decisions that are aligned with the Word and with church growth.
- Qualified church leaders defuse tensions rather than being in the middle of or instigating conflict.

4. **List other leader-qualifying characteristics described in verses 2 and 3 and share how they impact a maturing, Christ-centered church.**

- Husband of one wife.
- Hospitable.
- Able to teach.
- Not given to much wine.
- Not violent.
- Not greedy for money.
- Gentle.
- Not quarrelsome.
- Not covetous.

5. **How are the leader characteristics mentioned in verses 4 and 5 different from those in verses 1 through 3? Why is this significant?**

- Verses 4 and 5 deal with the character of a leader outside of the public eye.
- Qualified church leadership is measured in part by the conduct and behavior of those within the leader's closest circle: family.

- How can the leader's family not reflect the leader's character in the home?
- Who we really are can be hidden from public view, but the authentic person is revealed at home.

6. **The theme of verse 5 centers on how effective one is at managing their household as a qualifier for leadership. Is this a fair measure? Explain.**
   - Yes, it is. The home is the first place of love, priority, and genuine expression.

7. **Is a home led by fear and authority an indication that a person is effectively leading their household based on verses 4 and 5? Is the effective household the one that brings harmony with respected boundaries? Share your perspective on what makes for a Christ-centered household.**
   - The iron-fisted household is not a home filled with love and understanding.

8. **Do these verses disqualify a person from leadership if any member of their household is living an immoral or rebellious life?**
   - It depends on what the prospective leader is doing or has done to work through the issue.
   - Is the prospective leader an instigator or co-conspirator in the behavior?
   - The age or the emotional state of the person with undesirable behavior affects how much influence the leader may have on the unwelcomed behavior.

9. **Leadership qualifications continue in verses 6 and 7. Share how these requirements are important. (2 Timothy 2:24-26; 2 Corinthians 8:21)**
   - Not a novice. Experience is crucial in the wise handling of matters of spiritual importance and leading those who are immature with patient persistence built from love and practice.
   - An experienced leader knows how to call on wise counsel, understands the "why," and allows the Word of God to filter decisions. Such a leader is also unconcerned with popularity and is focused on making decisions that are rooted in love and righteousness.

- A qualified church leader has a good testimony and a good report from outsiders.

10. If a believer never plans to be a church leader, do the leadership standards still apply? (James 3:13, 17)

- Yes, standards of godliness and holiness always apply to all believers.
- Living a life that is wise in God's ways is honorable. Such a life displays a pattern of good works, pursues peace gently, is a considerate spirit, and demonstrates good works.

Unit I, Lesson 4
Answer Key
"What is Man?"
Psalm 8:1-9

Examining the Text

1. In verses 1 and 9, what is the writer attempting to describe when he uses "Lord, our Lord" to open this praise Psalm? What does he have with God?

- "Lord, our Lord" describes an owned and cherished relationship with the Highest.
- This acknowledgement makes the distinction that the praise is to God alone, that God is the One he calls.

2. What type of name does the Lord have, and how far is His name known? (vv. 1 and 9; Psalm 113:2; Romans 10:13; Philippians 2:9; Psalm 144:1-2)

- The Lord's name is majestic and blessed.
- The Lord is Savior.
- The Lord's name is known all over the earth

3. **The Lord is described as having a certain kind of name in verses 1 and 9. Why is this type of name so important? (Ecclesiastes 7:1; Proverbs 22:1)**

   - His majestic name is more valuable than costly perfume.

   - His majestic name is better than riches, silver, or gold.

4. **Why does David seem so awestruck and impressed in verses 3 and 4? (Genesis 1:26-28; Psalm 145:1-3; Hebrews 2:6-8; Psalm 144:3-4)**

   - David recognized the vastness of everything made, the work of God's hand, and the celestial skyscape (heavens), and it awed him to ponder why, with all the other creations, God is so focused on humankind.

   - The triune God (Father, Son, and Holy Spirit) created man in His image, to be like Him. That is why he placed man over the animals.

   - What makes mankind so special to warrant this much attention?

   - Are not the other created things more than spectacular? How amazing it is that that which was created without innate responses is so adored by God!

   - Christ is pleased when we agree with and love each other and work in unison.

5. **Where is man's placement in the order of beings created by God? In recognition of His position, what special things has the Lord given to man?**

   - God made man just a little lower than the angels.

   - Man is crowned with glory and honor.

   - All animals are under God's feet to give to man to manage and care for.

6. **What are the three distinct domains for the things listed that man is to have rule over? (vv. 6-8)**

   - The land (field), the air, and the sea (waters).

7. **After reviewing verses 6-8, how can we be better stewards over this charge?**

   - Care for the earth in part by reducing our carbon footprint and waste.

   - Replenish what we use.

   - Get out and enjoy nature's beauty.

8. **In what verses do we find references to God having body parts? What are those parts and what are they doing collectively? (KJV)**

   - Fingers in verse 3.

   - Hands and feet in verse 6.

   - Collectively, God's figurative body parts are working, creating, and ordering His creation.

Unit I, Lesson 5
Answer Key
"Whom Will You Feed?"
John 21:1-19

Examining the Text

1. **What happened in verse 6 that showed what can happen when we listen to the correct voice at the right time based on trust and obedience? What can we learn from this?**

   - The men cast their nets to exactly where they were told, and the fish haul was more than enough, filling two boats.

   - Their net did not break so that not one fish was lost. *(Discussion Spotlight)*

   - They were forced to get out of the comfort of their boats to bring in the abundance that required the hands of every disciple on board. They had to get into the water to bring in their overly abundant fish haul.

- Our lesson from this is that what awaits us when operating in God's will is greater than we can imagine or anticipate. Properly positioning ourselves, we may need help to take in the abundance that God has planned for our lives.

2. **When Jesus appeared to the disciples, was it apparent who He was? (v. 7) Among the group, who identified Jesus and what may have helped him recognize that it was the Lord speaking to them? (John 20:2; Luke 5:1-11)**

- None of the disciples recognized Jesus, except John.
- Some believe that Jesus's outward appearance starkly changed after His resurrection. Others claim that the early morning low light made it difficult to identify Him from the distance between the sea and the shoreline.
- John, the disciple whom Jesus loved, was the only one who identified Jesus.
- In John 20:2, it was the disciple whom Jesus loved who ran to the empty tomb with Peter.
- An earlier, similarly unsuccessful overnight fishing trip is recounted in Luke 5:1-11. The same three men first heard Jesus preach and received instructions for where to cast their nets. Here, too, they had an overloaded bounty that overtook their net and nearly filled two boats. As this event, leaving everything behind, they became followers of Christ, fishers of men.
- Now, Jesus repeated the miracle.

3. **In verse 12, what were the disciples fearful of doing, despite having clear knowledge? How can we take the question that they would not ask and use it in our own daily prayer life?**

- The disciples were afraid to ask Jesus who He was, because they did not recognize Him as they sat eating breakfast with Him.
- We should ask Jesus who He is daily, as an expression of seeking for Him to be a very present part of each day. We should want Him to define what part of His essence should ring true in our lives, today. Asking this question each day allows Christ to give us new, unexpected revelation and insight.

- The question not asked may be a missed opportunity for revelation, spiritual discernment, or ministry and blessings opportunities. Some matters require spiritual answers beyond the natural.

- Fear of standing out or asking in a time of need may cause us to miss our moment.

4. **After climbing ashore, what were the men specifically conscious of doing with their abundant blessing that Jesus miraculously made happen? (v. 11)**

- They counted their miraculous blessing: all 153 fish that were brought to them.

- We too, if possible, should count our blessings daily.

- They inspected their nets, noting that the same instrument, their net, which caught nothing before Jesus arrived was the same instrument that was strong enough for the overflow without breaking.

- When the Lord opens a bounty, we should never fear breaking what holds His blessings. Our focus should be on retrieving His entire blessing and then sharing the blessing.

5. **Now, Jesus directs His words to only one disciple among the others present. To whom did Jesus direct His words in verses 15-17? And, why to him? (Matthew 26:33-35; 16:18-20)**

- Jesus directed His words to Peter.

- Peter had denied Christ three times, as Jesus had predicted.

- Peter loved Jesus but had fallen in critical moments from fear for his life.

- Peter needed to know that he was forgiven.

- Peter needed another chance to express his love for Jesus directly, with the other disciples present.

- He needed restoration and encouragement to know that he was loved and included.

- As well, Jesus was giving Peter an assignment to love and care for all believers.

- This is the same Peter who was given the nickname "Rock," or "Cephas," upon whom His church would be built.

6. **How many times did Jesus ask Peter if he loved Him, and earlier during His Passion, how many times did Peter deny knowing Him? (John 13:36-38)**

   - Jesus asked Peter three times if he loved Him, one time for each time that Peter earlier denied knowing Him.

   - The number three signifies completeness, divine fullness, and perfection.

   - The significance of the number three is seen throughout the Bible: Jesus rose from the dead on the third day, the Holy Trinity/Godhead, Jesus prays in the Garden of Gethsemane three times, and the Magi's three gifts.

7. **Each time Jesus asked Peter about his love, He gave him a specific task to do based on that love. Name each of the tasks and note the differences. (vv. 15-17; Acts 20:27-28)**

   - "Feed My lambs": nourish the young in Christ.

   - "Tend My sheep": watch and oversee the believers, the church.

   - "Feed My sheep": always provide God's Word consistently, with assurance to believers.

8. **What was Peter's verbal response each time Jesus questioned him in verses 15-17?**

   - Each time, Peter said, "*You know* that I love you" (emphasis added), even if others doubted it because of his earlier denials.

   - Peter responded each time using the Greek word *phileo*, or brotherly love.

   - This conversation was 1) a deep internal assurance of Peter's love for Jesus; 2) a transparent public acknowledgement of that love; and 3) a willingness to be an instrument of this love in whatever he is being called to undertake.

Discussion Spotlight: Three types of love expressed in vv.15 -17

> 1. *Agape love is volitional, self-sacrificial love. Do you love Jesus more than anyone else? This is referring to the other disciple who was nearby. "If you do, feed My lambs." Our love should cause us to express it, to put feeling into action that meets needs (Hebrews 13:20-21).*

2. ***Second Time (v. 16)*** *– Agape love is volitional, self-sacrificial love. Do you love Jesus with all certainty? It is a love that is not in comparison to or on par with love for others, but is above our love for others. Essentially, be a protector and a caretaker for what Jesus is placing in your ministerial care.*

3. ***Third Time (v. 17)*** *– Phileo love is affection, affinity, or brotherly love. Again, do you love Jesus now that He has asked you to do something of great importance? Your new assignment will require that you give what is needed to sustain life and enable growth.*

9. **How did Peter feel about being asked the nearly identical question three times in succession in front of the other disciples? Why would Jesus continue to ask Peter the same question?**

- Peter was frustrated and grieved, as if his love for Jesus was in question.

- At times, for extra emphasis, repetition is needed to make an important point.

- The conversation reconnects Jesus's and Peter's love and bond despite Peter's earlier denials.

- Peter was then given a task, which showed that he was not only forgiven, but he was called.

- Peter's denials did not disqualify him nor nullify his calling to be a "fisher of men". (Luke 5:10)

- When Jesus challenges us deeply, it is never about our feelings, though He understands them. It is all about our purpose, our priorities, and our praise. It is how He can get us to the greatest intended place(s) that He intends for us.

Unit I, Lesson 6
Answer Key:
"The Start of Every Fight"
James 4:1-2

Why do we fight?

- To protect, destroy, eliminate, damage, get revenge, take from another, establish dominance or rule
- For recreation or entertainment
- As an aggressive emotional response to a perceived threat
- For survival
- To establish limits on personal and emotional space and needs
- As a result of a mismatch of preferences
- To display or distinguish skill, as a warning to others who may consider testing us

Examining the Text

1. **Verse 1 describes the place where fights with others begin. From where do they come?**

   - Unmet inner desires.
   - Emptiness that toils on our inside.
   - Lust or coveting something we strongly desire or think we should have.
   - Living by the world's standards for gain.
   - Envy and jealousy.
   - Greed.
   - Hatred.
   - Sin.
   - Selfishness.
   - Confusion.

2. **Name a few of the consequences that can result from a fight with another person. (Include verbal, physical or virtual fights.)** *Discussion Spotlight*

3. **How does James describe this inner issue that leads to fights with others. What can this mean? (1 Peter 2:11; Romans 7:14-15)**

    ●   Fights begin with an internal war or a battle, which must not be fought with our own strength.

    ●   The war is rooted in worldly lusts.

    ●   While we may have the desire to do what is right, our carnal spirit rages for what we think is missing according to a different, worldly standard of living.

    ●   Conflict with others stems from conflicted within one's self.

4. **How does Paul describe the change needed to overcome the carnal ways that lead us into conflicts? (Romans 12:2; 13:14; Proverbs 15:1-2)**

    ●   Renewing our minds will transform us to live the way God expects.

    ●   We must "put on" Christ to cover any sinful openings to the flesh and its lusts.

    ●   "A soft answer turns away wrath."

5. **For those who do not have what they desire after asking for it, James gives a reason why in verse 4. What is that reason? Explain.**

    ●   We do not get what we ask for because of wrong motives.

    ●   Anything that does not glorify God is of lower value.

    ●   If what we request is at the expense of someone else or may cause harm or conflict, then that request may not be of merit.

    ●   If we ask for prosperity, for what reason? If we ask for position, for what purpose?

    ●   Why not pray and ask for grace, peace, discernment, gratitude, and love?

6. **Galatians 5:19-21 describes the unfruitful yields that come from a life rooted in a worldly sinful nature. What are they?**
   - Unfruitful yields include sexual immorality, impurity, lustful pleasures, idolatry, sorcery, hostility, quarreling, jealousy, outbursts of anger, selfish ambition, dissension, division, envy, drunkenness, wild parties, and other sins

7. **In contrast to verses 19-21, Galatians 5:22 describes the yielded fruit that comes from a Holy Spirit-filled life. What are the "fruits of the spirit?**
   - The fruitful yields are love, joy, peace, patience, kindness, goodness, and faithfulness.

8. **If we find ourselves desiring to fight others, what are some ways for us to contend with that spiritual issue? (Romans 12:10, 13, 15-16; 1 Peter 3:11; Philippians 2:3-4)**
   - Love each other genuinely.
   - Be ready to help and be eager to practice hospitality.
   - Rejoice with others who are rejoicing and weep with others who are weeping.
   - Live in harmony with others, even ordinary people.
   - Do not be divisive, and do not be a know-it-all.
   - Put the needs of others first and value others above self.
   - Do nothing out of vain selfish ambition or conceit.
   - Atone for wrongdoings and find a way for reconciliation.
   - Pray for peace and work for it actively; make peace with enemies.
   - Make an effort to do what leads to peace; be a problem-solver.
   - Reconcile others to God.

9. **Is there a time when fighting is expected? (1 Timothy 6:12; 2 Timothy 4:7-8; 1 Peter 5:8-9; Ephesians 6:11-18; Romans 14:17-19; Jude 3-4)**

- Yes, sometimes fighting is expected – spiritual fighting.

- Fight the good fight for true faith.

- Paul says he "fought a good fight" and finished his race. We should be valiant contenders for the faith and for our ministries.

- The enemy is seeking whom he can devour.

- Put on the whole armor of God to stand against the enemy's wicked devices and schemes.

- We wrestle not against flesh and blood but against principalities, powers, the rulers of the darkness of this age, and spiritual hosts of wickedness in the heavenly places.

Discussion Spotlight: What will reduce or eliminate our desire to fight

- *Regular study and mediation in God's Word.,*

- *Physical and emotional security, recognizing that being right is not always important*

- *Our willingness to seek and work for peace.*

- *Proactive pausing, listening, and understanding, and choosing wisely when to stay and when to leave.*

- *Making personal joy a priority*

- *Seeking emotional support or therapy.*

- *Answering softly, which turns away wrath.*

- *Wisdom and discernment.*

- *Having blinders so that we are content with what we have*

- *Setting our own goals and communicating them clearly and consistently.*

- *Eliminating people-pleasing that isn't Holy Spirit-led.*

- *Prayer and meditation.*

- *Working toward life balance and communicating it.*

- *Making time to relax.*

- *Loving ourselves by seeing ourselves as God sees us; healthy self-love.*

- *Learning and practicing saying no, and standing firm in it.*

- *Finding the joy and beauty in others and not just focusing on their shortcomings.*

- *Seeking God's face for our lives.*

- *Accepting the beginning and ending of relationships, opportunities, and life stages.*

- *Simplicity.*

- *Patience.*

- *Lovingkindness.*

- *Longsuffering.*

- *Mercy.*

- *Forgiveness.*

- *Generosity.*

- *Gentleness.*

- *Self-control.*

- *Experience.*

- *Humility.*

Unit II, Lesson 1
Answer Key
"Man, Where Are You?"
Genesis 3:9

Examining the Text

1. From how many trees was Adam told that he could eat? (v. 2:16-17)

- Adam and Eve could eat from a large and abundant number of trees in the Garden of Eden, every tree except the Tree of the Knowledge of Good and Evil.

- One other tree is mentioned in verse 9: The Tree of Life., which Adam and Eve never got a chance to taste. It was not on the forbidden list, but after they ate from the Tree of the Knowledge of Good and Evil, God took the opportunity away from them by banishing them from the Garden.

2. If Adam and Eve ate from the Tree of the Knowledge of Good and Evil, what did the serpent promise them that was contrary to God's command? (v. 2:17)

- The serpent promised Adam and Eve (vv. 4-5) that if they ate of that fruit, then 1) they would not die; 2) their eyes would be opened; and 3) they would be like gods with the ability to know good and evil.

- Promise One was untrue – death is separation and sin separates man from God. Also, they would ultimately experience a physical death. Promise Two was true, but the details surrounding what it meant were hidden. Promise Three was partly true. No, they would not become gods because there is only one true God. Yes, they would know good and evil, but the destructive facts embedded in evil were not revealed.

- Half-truths are untruths and they are contrary to what God commands.

Discussion Spotlight: Connect the incident in the Garden of Eden with our own daily living, thoughts and actions. Were the other trees so familiar, plain or unpleasant in taste, so lacking in appeal, that Adam and Eve were enticed to try the one tree they were not permitted to eat from? How does this situation resonate with us as we consider what we do not have?

- *Everything that God made was good. God provided abundant variety and the selections were satisfying.*

- *Unquenched, we seem to always want more, different, better. We want what we cannot or should not have. We believe one little taste of what is forbidden will not hurt us.*
  - *But we must not have a Brill Cream faith that thinks "A little dab will do ya."*

- *A change in the normal routine of a relationship is a sign of a change in priority or desire.*

3. **How are we also like Adam and Eve when it comes to the things that we have been already blessed with and our attraction for the things we do not have?**

   - Our attention spans can be short and easily distracted.

   - That which we do not have can seem so attractive and inviting.

   - At times, we listen to voices that actually mean us harm.

   - Our familiarity with what we have can cause us to take what we have for granted, overlook its value, and forget the sacrifices that were made to obtain it.

   - Unexpected pain can arise when we step away from promises and commitments we have made to others.

4. **When God asked Adam, "Where are you?", could He have been seeking to know more than just Adam's physical location? Share your perspective.**

   - Some would say yes, because Adam and Eve had hidden themselves when God called for them during His usual evening stroll through the Garden. They were not in their familiar location.

   - With certainty, God knew exactly where Adam was hiding just like He knows exactly where we are, physically and spiritually. Do we not serve a God who is omnipresent (all-present) and omniscient (all-knowing)? Oh yes, we do! Praise God!

   - It is believed that, most importantly, God wanted to know where Adam was spiritually in their relationship. Was there a change they needed to discuss?

   - It can be assumed that God longed for His friend, Adam. He longs to have a relationship with us, too (Revelation 3:20).

5. **What did Adam and Eve's sin lead them to do?**

   - Adam and Eve covered themselves and tried to hide from God.

   - They ignored God's loving, familiar voice.

   - They became consumed with fear.

   - Sin is generally rooted in greed, selfishness, anger, jealousy, immoral thinking, hatred, and pride.

6. **How do we know that God seeks a whole relationship with humanity? (Psalm 8:4-6; Acts 4:27; 1 John 3:1; Colossians 3:12; Deuteronomy 6:4-5)**

   - God is mindful of mankind. He visits with mankind. God has provided position, power, and purpose for mankind.

   - God bestowed love upon us, and He calls us His sons and daughters.

   - We are God's elect, holy and deeply loved.

   - We are urged to place God's love in our hearts and to teach our descendants about His love on every occasion.

   - God gave His very best for a sin-sick creation.

   - God provided repentance and reconciliation because He wants us fully restored.

   - Mankind is God's only creation that does not operate innately. We have the capacity to express love in its highest form: by worshipping and obeying God.

   - Am I pursuing God?

   - Am I being consistent in my relationship with God?

   - Do I want to hear from Him?

   - Am I doing all of the talking in my private communing time with Him?

   - Right now, what am I pursuing with His leadership?

   - What is keeping me from having the best possible relationship with God?

7. **Like Adam and Eve, what does it mean to have our eyes opened? (v. 7, James 1:14-16)**

   - Opened eyes means having an unfiltered view of things that may not be in our best interests.

   - Losing innocence that cannot be recaptured.

   - Adam discovered information that had not previously been revealed to him: his nakedness.

   - Having eyes opened may also mean that new desires are opened, like a gateway to damaging or unnatural attractions.

   - The seed for unhealthy desires, passions, and priorities may be awakened.

8. **Beginning at Genesis 3:11, do we find the serpent speaking while God was confronting Adam about his sin, or after? Is this an observation to be noted when we are enticed by others?**

- The serpent was silent and satisfied with his chaos and destruction.
- Adam and Eve were left alone to deal with their revealed sin.
- Adam blamed Eve (the woman that God gave him, he says), Eve blamed the serpent, and the serpent accepted no responsibility.

9. **What tools can we add to our daily living to fight against sinful enticements? (1 Peter 2:11; 1 John 3:3; 1 Corinthians 6:18; Joshua 1:8; Hebrews 4:16; 2 Corinthians 7:1)**

- Stop lust, because it wages war against our souls.
- Fix our hearts on Christ.
- Don't gaze. Staring upon certain things too long begins the fantasizing process.
- Flee. It is best to remove ourselves from situations when we know it is not right.
- Meditate upon the Word of God, day and night. Observe all things in His Word.
- Think about what we will lose if we give in to lust.
- Be in prayer constantly.
- Cleanse ourselves from defilement; remove it from our lives.

Consider: **Ways to measure the strength of our relationship with God:**

A. How much time have I spent in God's presence, this week? Do I talk to Him daily?

B. Does my life routine make God a priority?

C. Am I actively engaged in what God desires for my life?

> **Colossians 3:17** – And whatever you do in word or deed, do all in the name of the Lord Jesus, giving thanks to God the Father through Him.

10. **Did Adam and Eve die when they ate the fruit?**

- Death means separation. Yes, they died spiritually.
- Satan never gives the full picture, the full extent of what we will lose if we pursue his "enticements."

Consider:

    A. What are indications that a relationship with another person is healthy?

    B. What are indications that a relationship with another person may be ruptured?

Indications that a relationship with another person is healthy:

- There is intentional proximity and frequent and honest communication, which show interest, concern and support.
- Shared goals that both parties contribute toward accomplishing.
- Sacrifice of time and resources.
- Appropriate, timely gifts.
- Fruit, evidence of something jointly produced.

Indications that a relationship with another person may be ruptured:

- Parties hide or only partially disclose important information with their significant other.
- One or both parties consistently find comfort with sharing primary relationship information with someone else outside of that primary relationship.
- One or both parties add new behaviors and conditions to the relationship that are neither nurturing to the relationship nor previously agreed upon.
- One or both parties engage in deceptive behavior, lies, lack of ownership for fault(s), and poor choices.
- There are unaccounted for time gaps.
- One or both parties spend an inordinate amount of attention on other interests or priorities outside of the relationship.

- One or both partners respond with an indifferent tone or a tone that is unwarranted, inappropriate, or awkward for the situation.

> **Unit II, Lesson 2**
> **Answer Key**
> **"Get Off the Fence!"**
> **1 Kings 18:21**

Examining the Text

1. **Under what harsh environmental conditions were the people suffering? Why? (1 Kings 17:1)**

   - There was a severe drought in the land.

   - God, through Elijah, brought a drought that affected both humankind and livestock.

2. **What kind of king was Ahab? (16:30, 33)**

   - Ahab was the son of King Omri (reigned 12 years; created the city Samaria), an evil king who patterned his lifestyle after King Jeroboam. He was an idol worshipper.

   - Ahab did evil in God's eyes, more so than any king before him.

   - He married Jezebel, daughter of King Ethbaal of Sidon.

   - He worshipped Baal after marrying Jezebel.

   - Ahab built a temple and an alter for Baal in Samaria.

   - He set up a Asherah pole (sacred tree or pole that stood at Canaanite religious locations honoring the pagan fertility goddess Asherah).

   - Ahab did more to provoke God's anger than any king before him (v. 33).

   - Ahab was king of Israel (the Northern Kingdom with ten tribes of Israel) for 22 years. He reigned while Asa was king of Judah (the Southern Kingdom with two tribes: Judah and Benjamin). Israel was divided after King Solomon's reign.

Discussion Spotlight: What do we know about the Israelites' spiritual condition?

3. **What does it mean to waver or hobble between opinions? (v. 21)**

   - A person is unable to make a spiritual choice, so they sample life from among both the Godly and ungodly.

   - A person who has lukewarm faith (Revelation. 3:15-18). Laodicea had poor water from Roman aqueducts. Hot spring, mineral-rich water came from Hierapolis in the north; while cool, snowmelt, refreshing water came from the Colossae in the south.

   - A carnal Christian, unable to choose a life that is sold out to Christ. They may display spiritual characteristics but are unable to give up the world and its ways.

4. **Name things or issues that can cause a person to stumble back and forth between the spiritual and carnal worlds.**

   - Lack of repentance.

   - The type of relationships a person maintains in their life.

   - Joy in sinning.

   - Fear of giving up something that is not good but provides a temporary or slow detrimental pleasure.

   - Selfishness; lack of concern for how their actions affect others.

   - Belief that a sin issue is only temporary and will be given up soon. Belief that they are in full control and can stop the sin lifestyle whenever they choose.

   - Lack of Word-based guidance, weak spiritual grounding, poor spiritual depth, and immaturity.

   - People-pleasing; unable to say no. The person's mindset is guided by the expedient.

   - Addiction.

   - Emotional scars and unresolved trauma.

5. **When Elijah challenged the people with his question, what was their response? What could have been the reasons for their response? (v. 21)**

- The people responded with total silence.
- They were not convinced they needed to change.
- Despite enduring a drought, their God relationship had not yet become treasured and personal.
- There was a "group think" issue. No one wanted to stand out by standing up. The majority is not always right.
- Elijah was a prophet and representative of a mighty God, but he was an enemy of the state. He was considered a troublemaker and, likely, the people were fearful of being viewed as Elijah-sympathizers. The people should have been more interested in being God-sympathizers in a drought-stricken land with an evil, idol-worshiping king.

6. **When seeing God's awesome power on display compared to silence from the idol gods, despite the pagan priests' pleading all day for their idol gods to appear, how did the people respond then? (v. 39)**

- The people fell on their faces and cried out, "The Lord—he is God! Yes, the Lord is God!"
- The power of the true and living God produced a clear, resounding response from His people.
- The people had a chance to compare the difference in power and authority between the true and living God and the false, powerless, pagan gods.

7. **What personal idols might we have that may be affecting our spiritual growth?**

- Stuff.
- People.

- Status/Popularity.
- Power/Position.
- Ego/Opinions.
- Pre-occupation/concern about others' opinions.

Discussion Spotlight: *<u>A sinful life</u> can make us believe our wrongdoing will not be discovered. It produces a sense of low accountability for our words or deeds. Even more, we may demand others to endorse our behavior without question, complaint, or judgment. This attitude shows a lack of shame, contrition, or humility.*

Elijah's Altar

- *Using twelve stones, one for each tribe of Israel, Elijah rebuilt the destroyed altar (v. 30).*
- *Elijah dedicated it in the name of the Lord.*
- *He dug a trench around the altar to prepare for the overflow.*
- *He then put wood on the altar at a proper supply for igniting and holding a fire.*
- *Elijah cut open a sacrificial bull and laid it on the altar. Something valuable must be cut for change to occur.*
- *Three times Elijah filled four jars with water and poured the water on the sacrifice and the wood.*
- *The overflowing water ran around the alter and filled the trench.*
- *Elijah then called unto the Lord, acknowledging God's presence and his relationship to Him as a servant.*
- *Elijah then asked God to answer so that the people would know that "You, Oh Lord, are God, and that you have turned their hearts back" (v. 37).*
- *Fire from heaven fell upon the altar and consumed the offering, wood, the stones, and the dust, and it licked up the water in the trench (v. 38).*

The People's Response

- *They fell on their faces and proclaimed, "The Lord, He is God; the Lord He is God" (v. 39).*

Elijah's Response

- *He ordered all of Baal's false prophets to be seized and executed at the Kishon Brook.*
- *He sent Ahab to go eat and drink because the drought was ending.*
- *He went to the top of Mt. Carmel and bowed with his head between his knees. God had him to look to the sea seven times.*
- *A great rain fell (v. 45).*

Drought

- *Lack of rain over an extended period causes living things to die or retreat into hibernation.*
- *The Dust Bowl of 1934 is considered the greatest U.S. drought. It lasted almost ten years and affected eighty percent of the continental U.S.*
- *In a severe drought, the ground cracks open, animals' lifecycles and innate habits are disrupted, and vegetation browns and withers.*
- *The start and end of a drought cannot be known.*
- *Drought takes away growth cycles and fruit-bearing seasons.*
- *Water must be drawn from difficult places, such as the ground and distant sources.*
- *In terms of our reaction to drought, it causes one to be resourceful with what remains and to eliminate wasteful tendencies. Also, infighting tends to arise.*
- *Other drought types include creativity (e.g., writer's block), relationships (e.g., due to incompatibility, disagreements), and emotional wounds (e.g., depression, trauma response).*

> **Unit II, Lesson 3**
> **Answer Key**
> **"Lord, Where Are You?"**
> **Matthew 2:2**

Examining the Text

1. **What did the Magi seek to do when they arrived in Jerusalem and appeared before King Herod? (v. 2)**

   - The Magi sought information about the new King's' location.
   - The Magi wanted to worship the newborn King.

2. **How did King Herod react to these strangers' (the Magi's) request? (v. 3)**

   - Kind Herod and all of Jerusalem were troubled, deeply concerned.

3. **Having concerns about the reported newborn King, Jesus, whom did Herod send to investigate the issue, and what might this say about the Herod's leadership? (vv. 7-8)**

   - Herod sent the Magi on their way with an order that they check out the issue and return to him to report what they found.
     - ◊ Some matters are so serious that they cannot be delegated, and certainly not to strangers.
     - ◊ However, believing his future place as king was at stake, Herod did not send his own people to investigate the matter.
   - Incompetent people around you can cost you.
     - ◊ Herod had no idea if the Magi are trustworthy, and he did not know when they would return.
     - ◊ Likely, Herod did not want to arouse suspicion by sending official royal investigators.
       - ◊ Perhaps Herod did not have people around him who were astute enough to see the celestial sign.

◊ Perhaps Herod did not have informed and valued advisors to properly counsel him about what to do.

4. **When the Magi saw the Christ Child, what two key actions did they perform that we are to replicate in our spiritual lives? (v. 11)**

- The Magi fell down and worshipped Him. They knew He was worthy of all the praise.

- The Magi gave Him gifts of gold, frankincense, and myrrh—resources needed for His family's travels to Egypt.

Things we can ask ourselves as we ponder the Magi's pursuit of worship:

- *How far are we willing to go for a worship experience?*

- *What are we willing to leave behind to have an encounter with God?*

- *What are we willing to bring to the worship ex*perience?

5. **When it was time to leave, what did the Magi do? Why? What can we learn from their example? (v. 12)**

- God spoke to the Magi in a dream that persuaded them to take a different route home. God gave them a sign to not return to Herod.

    ◊ They did not have to report back to Herod, which spared the Christ Child's life.

    ◊ They possibly spared their own lives.

    ◊ Their decision provided more time for Mary and Joseph to escape.

    ◊ They likely had to take a longer route home. We may need to change our personal routes. With God giving us a new path, we may avoid potential troubles that await us.

- Allow the Lord to *guide our path*. Listen to the Holy Spirit's *voice of instruction*. Be *willing to change course*.

6. **How much effort do we really put into pursuing God?**

- Is my relationship with God at its best when we allow others in our lives to do all the pursuing? For example:
  ◊ Others do the praying, while we wait for the answers.
  ◊ Others do the studying, while we wait for whatever Word is shared as the exclusive time we spend in God's Word.
  ◊ Others do the sacrificing, while we relegate ourselves to being cheerleaders or spectators.
  ◊ Others do the witnessing, while we just hope to avoid it and never prepare to share our own testimonies.
  ◊ Others are transparent in relationships with spiritual family, while we keep it surface level to avoid discussing our shortcomings, struggles, or lack of study.

7. **Are we tempted to give up when our respective journeys are not what we expected? Explain.**

- (Personal responses here.)

8. **What would be examples or evidence that we are choosing to pursue God in our lives? (Jeremiah 29:13-14; John 14:21)**

- Asking God to reveal His will for our lives.
- A consistent and intentional prayer life that draws us closer to God's will and way.
- Reading God's Word with intent and clarity.
- Regular worship and participation in ministry.
- Inviting and nurturing quality friendships, asking God to provide ways to connect with likeminded fellow believers.
- Reading books that are biblically sound, spiritually fulfilling, and life-changing, books from reputable Christian authors.

- Inviting the Holy Spirit into every decision.
- Asking God to cultivate whatever fruit of the spirit we will need for each day.
- Obedience to God, living in accordance with His Word.
- Serving others by sharing our time and resources, and by giving encouraging words.

9. **Provide illustrations of behaviors and actions that demonstrate that man is pursuing the interests of man? (E.g., greed)**

- Greed.
- Sexual immorality.
- Violence and destruction.
- Selfishness.
- Excess.
- Abusive power.
- Approval-seeking for hollow validation.
- Obsessive desire for fame and notoriety.
- Hardened ways and heart; no remorse.

Unit II, Lesson 4
Answer Key
"Is There Anything God Cannot Do?"
Matthew 8:27

Examining the Text

1. **Has there been an event or situation in your life that was simply beyond words?**

- The election and re-election of President Barak Obama and witnessing his inauguration in-person both times.
- The birth of my children.

- The survival of two of my children who were sick at birth.
- The discovery of my birth father when I was 46 years old. Unbeknownst to me, he lived just two blocks from where I purchased my first home, where I lived for thirteen years never knowing he existed.

2. **Before the miracle, what was the disciples' greatest concern? (v. 25)**

- The men feared death at sea.
- The men were anxious about battling something greater than their level of strength and control could endure.
- What belonged outside of their boat – water -- was now coming into their boat at a rate faster than they could handle.

3. **What was Jesus' greatest concern for His disciples? (v. 26)**

- The disciples were gripped by their fears, causing them to lose hope and assurance.
- The size of their faith was too small despite Jesus's riding in the adversity with them.
- They finally went to get the Master when they were convinced they would not survive the storm. Are we using God only as a last resort, an EMT or trauma specialist?
- Fear and faith cannot jointly abide (Hebrews 11:1).

Discussion Spotlight: What happens when we are overcome with fear? How can we overcome these feelings?

4. **When asking what manner or type of man Jesus was, were they questioning who He is (His background), the extent of His power, the source of His power, or something else?**

- The *extent of Jesus's power*: What can He not do? Did He really just do that? Jesus's capability and power have no limit or constraint.
- The <u>*source of Jesus's power*</u>: How did He just do that?

- The disciples had seen Jesus's power displayed before, yet they were all in awe when it benefited them directly. He and the Father are one.
- *Who was He?* (Jesus's background.) It was as if they were questioning who He was despite walking with Him, sitting at His feet, and witnessing all His other miracles. Clearly, He was more than a just carpenter from Nazareth.

5. **Provide a personal experience of witnessing something that seemed to defy reality or human capability?**

- My car was sliding sideways to a certain accident on a slick and snowy street, but somehow my car missed every possible object.
- Witnessing the speed, agility, strength, and stamina of professional athletes.

6. **What manner of God do we serve? (Describe Him by what He has done or is doing for you.)**

- God is *all-knowing, all-seeing, and ever-present.* No one has anything over Him.
- Our God *created all things* that were made and there is not anything made that He did not make.
- God gave His very best for the sake of love; He gave Himself willingly for love.
- God provided *a path to salvation* for a stiff-necked, disobedient people.
- *God is patient and kind.*
- *God uses the unusable.*
- *God sees hope in the hopeless.*
- *God plants gifts in the undeserving.*
- *God made man the crown of His creation,* yet man was given free will to choose to love Him back.
- *God is thrilled by our praise* and *deserves to be exalted* above all things.
- *God has a plan for His people.*
- *God upholds every promise* He has made.

- *God sustains all life* and needs no rest or replenishment.

- *God places a hedge of protection around us*, but He is willing to leave the 99 to *retrieve the one who is lost.*

- <u>*God is our rock* when all other ground is sinking sand.</u>

- *God is the One.* Jesus is the Way, the Truth, and the Life.

7. **What life questions are you facing that only an all-powerful, all-loving God can handle?**

   - He is a God of great, miraculous things.

   - Eyes have not seen, ears have not heard, neither has it entered into the hearts of men all that our God will do. We can't fully imagine His greatness (1 Corinthians 2:9).

8. **How do our actions demonstrate our knowledge of Christ's power over whatever challenges we are facing?**

   - Our trust in Christ's power *holds firm in situations of crisis or uncertainty.*

   - Our first response to adversity is to be and do *what Christ expects and not what man expects.*

   - In error, we try to seek the opinions of others to validate what God has already told us.

   - We are to *live out the Word of God by seeking righteousness.*

   - We are required to *guide others in God's Word.*

   - Our motive is to <u>*be a servant, first.*</u>

Discussion Spotlight: What is God to you?

Unit II, Lesson 5
Answer Key
"It's Not What They Call You"
Matthew 16:13

Examining the Text

1. **What did Jesus ask His disciples privately in verse 13? What were their responses?**

   - Jesus asked His disciples who did people say He was. They gave three different answers: John the Baptist, Elijah, and Jeremiah.

   - *John the Baptist:* Jesus's cousin. A prophet and a fearless forerunner announcing Jesus's coming. He preached repentance. He was odd in appearance and ministered in a wasteland location. He confronted King Herod about his sinful illegal marriage to Herodias.

   - *Elijah.* The most famous of the prophets. He predicted the start and the end of a three-year drought. He restored a dead child to life. He appeared with Moses and Jesus at the New Testament transfiguration scene.

   - *Jeremiah.* The "weeping prophet." He wrote the Old Testament books of "Jeremiah" and "Lamentations." He preached to antagonistic and apathetic audiences who ignored him. He witnessed the people turning to idolatry against his warnings. He is a testament of faithfulness in God.

   - Jesus was not conducting a poll to gauge His notoriety or popularity based on what He did in chapter 15.

   - Jesus was not seeking to know what title or position others wanted to assign to Him. Titles meant nothing to Him. He was called and guided to perform a mission and ministry of salvation.

   - For some of us, who Jesus is to us could change daily based on what part of Himself is revealed.

2. **Describe and explain the difference between what Jesus asked them in verse 13 and what He asked in verse 15.**

   - Absolutely, there is a difference between the two questions. His second question, "Who do you say that I am?", indicated that He now wanted to know if they really knew Him for who and what He was/is.

   - The first question related to what the casual followers, who did not "know Him," were saying. The second question was a grounded, intimate question to those who were closest to His words, deeds, heart, and purpose.

   - Jesus wanted to know if His words and essence had penetrated their thoughts and if they felt His eternal love for them.

   - He also wanted to know if they were rightly aligned with Him,—not just because of the miracles like so many of the casual followers were. His disciples were convinced that He was/is the Messiah.

   - A Prophet will be sent (Malachi 4:5).

3. **How likely is it that we may be called something different based on an experience someone has had with us? Explain. Provide examples of ways that we may be identified by others who know us.**

   - It is very likely that what people call us will be based on what they have experienced with us.

   - People remember us from back when we may have been different.

   - People's views of us are based on a limited view of our relationships, talents, actions, or past.

   Discussion Spotlight: Provide examples of various ways we may be identified by others who know us.

   - *By what we do for a living.*
   - *By the things we say or how we say them.*
   - *By our affiliations or family.*
   - *By where we are from or where we live.*

- *By what we look like to them.*
- *By past events or by our actions.*
- *By our personality.*

Discussion Spotlight: We have all lost relationships because we either misidentified someone's character or they misidentified ours.

4. **Who responded to Jesus's question in verse 15 and what did he say? From your perspective, how did the one who responded come to his conclusion?**

- Peter, or Simon Bar-Jonah, spoke up: "Thou art the Christ, the Son of the Living God."
- Peter boldly proclaimed that the Person before him was, in fact, the Christos, the Anointed One, the Messiah, the One foretold, the manifestation of the Living God in human form, the humanity of the Divine.
- God revealed this to Peter. Enlightenment and wisdom are a higher level of thought and expression. There are words that only God gives us. We may not understand them, initially.
- Jesus called Simon Bar-Jonah blessed in the presence of the others, noting that "flesh and blood has not revealed this to you, but My Father in heaven."

5. **Let's reimagine the question in verse 13 and reshape it as if we are asking it to others around us. What would we ask?**

- Do people like me? Do you love me?
- What do others (family, friends, co-workers, and strangers) say about me?
- Do others know about my past?
- Do they know who I am? (Is it by titles, bloodline, accomplishments, etc.?)

6. **How does our experience with Jesus impact the way we serve Him, respond to Him, and seek to please Him?**

- It may be the very moment that saves our lives, our reputation, or a relationship.
- Encountering Jesus stops everything else.

- It is the reason, the "why," for our service.
- The motivation is not man-centered.

7. What is the difference between who you believed Jesus to be earlier in your Christian walk and who He is now?

- Before, it was all about what others said and expected – my parents, Sunday School teachers, etc. Now, I am self-motivated to study the Word of God, and I inspect what others say or share with me.
- Worshipping Jesus is no longer just a weekly activity on my calendar.
- I have experienced Jesus through situations that have allowed me to know He truly loves me and seeks the best for me.
- Before, I thought it was about following a set of "do's and don'ts," and now it is about living in a loving and abundant way to please the Lord.

8. Why do you praise Him and how? Why do you believe in Him and how? Why is He a priority and how? Why are you determined to serve Him and how? Because He is…

- Redeemer.
- Healer.
- Mind Regulator.
- Counselor.
- Comforter.
- Miracle Worker
- Restorer.
- Lover of my soul.

9. What were Jesus' instructions to His disciples in verse 20?

- Jesus said not to tell anyone He was the Christ. They needed to fully understand Him and His mission before widely sharing what they witnessed. Timing is important.

Powerful Questions in the Bible

A Study of God's Voice Speaking to His People

ADDITIONAL FACILITATOR RESOURCES

POWERFUL QUESTIONS IN THE BIBLE
A STUDY OF GOD'S VOICE SPEAKING TO HIS PEOPLE
Verse-by-verse interpretive study aid (Matthew 2:1-16)

V. 1

    a. Jesus is born in Bethlehem.

    b. Wisemen from the east arrive in Jerusalem. (Bethlehem is five miles downhill from Jerusalem. Bethlehem is now located in Palestinian territory.)

- Little is known about them.
- They traveled great distances, perhaps thousands of miles.
- They held high positions from the area of Parthia near Babylon.
- They may be Jews who stayed in Babylon after the Exile.
- They could have been eastern astrologers with copies of the Old Testament or other manuscripts.
- They could have been given a special message from God.
- Traditionally, it is thought there were three wisemen, but there could have been more.
- They were from different lands far away.
- They recognized Jesus from a distance, while those near, Jews, missed Him and His arrival altogether.

V. 2

    a. The wisemen wanted to know where they could find the Newborn King.

    b. They saw His star and were compelled to follow it to come worship Him.

V. 3

    a. Herod was disturbed about the news of a king and prominent men traveling from afar to behold and worship Him.

    b. Herod, the king, is troubled that the wisemen have arrived to worship the King of the Jews. His thoughts changed from curious concern to anger that someone might overtake his royal position without his knowledge.

V. 4

    a. Herod called a meeting and gathered his counsel of leaders—scribes and chief priests.

    b. He wanted to know where the King was born.

    c. We all have blinders and may miss obvious signs.

    d. How is it that Jesus spoke and performed miracles, yet so many missed His message?

    e. How could Pharaoh see and be affected by the plagues, yet he still missed it?

    f. How are we also placed in the same circumstance as others and flounder while they may flourish?

    g. How do two children in the same household yield two totally different life results?

V. 5

    a. The wisemen told the king that the birth was to be in Bethlehem based on the ancient prophecies (Micah 5:2).

    b. The Messiah had been anticipated for generations.

V. 6

    a. The prophesy.

V. 7

    a. Herod pulled the wisemen aside to ask when the star had appeared in the sky.

V. 8

   a. Herod "sent," or "gave his approval," for them to travel on to Bethlehem.

   b. They were to send word back to him when they found the Newborn King.

   c. Herod claimed to the wisemen that he intended to worship the new King.

   d. Some tasks cannot be delegated. Examples:

- Learning
- Listening
- Fruits of the spirit (Love, joy, Patience, kindness, gentleness, faithfulness, self-control)
- Worship
- Growth

V. 9

   a. The wisemen listened to the king's instruction and they departed to Bethlehem.

   b. The star guided their travels.

   c. The star was affixed right over the place where Jesus was.

V. 10

   a. They rejoiced as they arrived at the place where the star stood still over Jesus

V. 11

   a. What rewards did the wisemen receive by choosing to pursue Christ?

- They saw Mary and Jesus and fell down and worshipped the Newborn King.
- They worshipped at the feet of the Savior.
- They beheld Jesus, worshipped Him, and fellowshipped.
- They were in the glorious presence of the heavenly host.
- Their gifts were their best and provided what was needed for what Mary and Joesph would face later.

b. Being led by Christ

- Are we willing to take a different route when encountering Jesus?
- Are we willing to offer our best and know confidently that He never leaves us empty?
- Can we accept that following Jesus is a different path?
- Can we accept that He may cause us to leave valuable things behind for reasons we may not totally understand? Can we trust Him?
- Jesus gives true freedom, peace, joy, purpose, and life.

V. 13

a. An angel visited Joseph to warn him that Herod was seeking to kill Jesus and that he must flee to Egypt.

V. 14

a. Joseph got up in the middle of the night, packed up his family, and journeyed to Egypt.

V. 15

a. Joseph, Mary, and Jesus remained in Egypt until Herod died.

b. They stayed in the same land their ancestors had escaped from after 358 years of bondage.

V. 16

a. Herod discovered that he has been tricked by the wisemen. Clues, other than the star, of Jesus's whereabouts had disappeared.

b. Herod ordered all male children two-years old and younger to be put to death.

Verse-by-Verse Interpretive Study Aid (Matthew 8)

V. 1

    a. Enthralled crowds followed to hear more of Christ's words.

V. 2-4

    a. A leper is healed.

    b. The man was ostracized due to the unclean disease and could only have the priest confirm that he was now clean (Leviticus 13 through 14:2).

    c. The disease was thought to be given by God.

    d. The leper believed that Jesus could heal him.

V. 5-13

    ■ A Roman centurion seeks help for his servant who has palsy (a weakness disease).

    a. Help was sought for someone else, and healing occurred without the diseased person being present.

V. 14-15

    a. Peter's mother-in-law is healed of a fever with a touch from Jesus at her home.

V. 16

    a. Many sick and demon-possessed people are all healed.

V. 17

    a. Healings are the fulfillment of Scripture (Isaiah 53:4).

V. 19

    a. A scribe seeks to follow Jesus.

V. 27

    a. A well-known demon-possessed man is healed. Demons are sent into a herd of swine that run off a cliff into water and drown.

V. 34

    a. After the healings, the demon-possessed man and Jesus are thrown out of the city.

    b. Being "marveled" occurs twice in scripture:

- (v. 10) Jesus marvels at the centurion's faith.
- (v. 27) His disciples marvel over Jesus's miracle of calming the raging storm at sea.

POWERFUL QUESTIONS IN THE BIBLE
A STUDY OF GOD'S VOICE SPEAKING TO HIS PEOPLE
Student Experience Inventory

I pray that our time together to study God's voice though ***Powerful Questions*** has provided depth and enlightenment for your spiritual journey. Thank you for choosing to complete our study. Please answer the questions below, as we seek to grow from your learning experience and identify ways to improve this study.

1. Were the study materials: Too Demanding, Not Challenging Enough, or Just Right? (Circle your answer.)

2. In advance of each class, did you study the materials in preparation for the lessons taught? Yes or No. (Circle your answer.)

3. Were the weekly class sessions times: Too Long, Too Short, Just Right? (Circle your answer.)

4. How did the lesson(s) speak to you?

5. What new biblical insights did you gain during your study?

6. How will you put the lessons into action and practice?

7. How can we improve the Bible learning experience for you?

8. Did the facilitator share the lessons in way that was understandable? Yes or No. (Circle your answer.)

9. Was the facilitator well prepared for each lesson? Yes or No. (Circle your answer.)

10. Would you participate in another *Powerful Questions* session, if held? Yes or No. (Circle your answer.)

11. Any other thoughts you would like to share about the *Powerful Questions* study?

Additional *Powerful Questions*

Additional examples of Bible questions warrant careful consideration for a deeper personal study. Look for future *Powerful Questions in the Bible* study lessons.

Who/Whom?

- Isaiah 6:8 (ESV) – And I heard the voice of the Lord saying, "Whom shall I send, and who will go for us?"

What?

- Romans 8:31 (NIV) – What shall we then say to these things? If God be for us, who can be against us?

Where?

- Psalm 139:7 (NIV) – Where can I go from your Spirit? Where can I flee from your presence?
- Job 38:4 (ESV) – "Where were you when I laid the foundations of the earth?

How?

- Malachi 3:8 (ESV) – Will man rob God? Yet you are robbing me. But you say, 'How have we robbed you?'…

Why?

- Acts 9:4 (NLT) – He fell to the ground and heard a voice saying to him, "Saul! Saul! Why are you persecuting me?"

ACKNOWLEDGMENTS

★ ★ ★

With gratitude, I acknowledge my pastors for life: Rev. Bransford Utley, Rev. J.D. Marks, Rev. Joseph Trask, Rev. Larry Rascoe, Rev. Jeffery Johnson, Rev. Adrian M. Brooks, Rev. Robert Esters, Rev. George Madison, Rev. Jeff Allensworth, Rev. Dr. T.D. Stubblefield, Rev. Carlos Smith, Rev. Daryl Blanks, Rev. Dr. James Wilson and Rev. Damon Lynch, III. Further, I acknowledge my cherished teachers, who have rightly divided the Word of truth: Constance Kelly, Frank Newell, Rev. Steven Brown, and Rev. Dr. Luke Bobo.

Love acknowledgments to my wife and life partner, Lori Sutton; my beautiful children, Taryn, Quinn, Austin, and William; my parents, Walter and Jean Brown; and my special siblings whose unfailing love is unparalleled: Sadrid Sutton, Natosha Sutton, and Shawn Humphries.

Editors
Rev. Dr. T.D. Stubblefield, Dr. Kathy Hood Culmer, and Rev. Dr. Adrian Brooks

Proverbs 3: Every Day and in Every Way

#powerfulquestions #mountwings #winswithoutcheat

ABOUT THE AUTHOR

★ ★ ★

Royce Sutton lives in Cincinnati, Ohio, and he enjoys the beauty of the outdoors, writing, and public speaking about the powers of building wealth of the spirit, the mind, the body, and personal treasury. He is a God-revering servant and a life-long learner.

When speaking, Royce has been described as captivating, inspiring, passionate, and informed. He is available to be a speaker and train groups or leaders about leveraging the power of the moment through healthy, purposeful life choices. These choices, he believes, create unlimited possibilities for how we love, live, prosper, and transform the world.

Royce Sutton has been an elected official, is an investor targeting Black tech business growth, and has served on over forty organizations' boards of directors that include chambers of commerce, community foundations, finance committees, neighborhood revitalization, and economic justice. Also, Royce's efforts led to the creation of a community dental clinic for uninsured patients and a private charter school for at-risk students. He has served as an overseas missionary and been a lecturer at the university level. His church leadership spans from youth ministry, pastoral selection, operations director, trustee, and leading a multi-million dollar capital and building campaign. Royce is an ordained deacon and has been a Bible study facilitator for over twenty years.

With an over thirty-year, senior executive, financial services industry career in seven states, Royce has developed innovative capital investment strategies targeting underserved urban and rural areas. He has written financial education curriculum and lectured on the subject in numerous faith-based and community settings. Seeing an unmet need, he led the creation of a digital financial education tool that has reached over 1.2 million high school students. As the weekly featured guest on a leading St. Louis-based radio station, he shared valuable tips about how to make wise money choices.

Royce holds bachelor's and master's degrees from Indiana State University and a Community Development Certification from The University of Oklahoma. He is married to Lori Sutton and a father to four beautiful, uniquely talented children.

Royce Sutton's other written works:

- *Never Miss These Critical Life Appointments: The Keys to Success, Longevity and Fulfillment*
- *30 Days After 30 Years: A Relaunch for Life's Next Stage*
- *When Your Ends Don't Meet: Learning How to Break the Cycle of Debt and Building Wealth*

Contact

realroyce4@gmail.com
Instagram: roycebelieves
LinkedIn: Royce Sutton
PowerfulQuestions-RoyceSutton.com

Made in the USA
Columbia, SC
19 September 2024

42642651R00089